THE THIN LINE:
A Review of Leadership Thought and Practice
Volume 6

THE THIN LINE

CONTRIBUTORS:

Jonathan Acuff	Jason Locy	Mandy and Brian Miller	Carmen Vaught
Jon Adams	Brad Lomenick	Mark A. Noll	Kay Warren
Francis Chan	Gabe Lyons	John Ortberg	Carlos Whittaker
Margaret Feinberg	Brett McCracken	John Piper	Dallas Willard
Reggie Joiner	Jedd Medefind	Mike Sares	Timothy Willard
Timothy Keller	Jonathan Merritt	Andy Stanley	Jason Young

A CATALYST LEADER IS:
INTENTIONAL ABOUT COMMUNITY
ENGAGED IN CULTURE
UNCOMPROMISING IN INTEGRITY
PASSIONATE ABOUT GOD
COURAGEOUS IN CALLING
AUTHENTIC IN INFLUENCE

WITH THE COLLABORATION OF MANY CULTURALLY-ENGAGED LEADERS AND BELIEVERS, WE SEEK TO EXPLORE SOME VERY FUNDAMENTAL, YET CRITICAL, IDEAS OF CULTURE, FUTURE, CHURCH, GOSPEL.

UTILIZING THIS REVIEW: This year's volume has been designed to be effective for both individual and group study. At the end of the book, you'll find discussion questions to help you incorporate *The Thin Line's* content into your small group or leadership team meetings. Use these questions as a starting point but we would also encourage you to bring your own questions to the group and explore these ideas together. Conversation is a starting point to form true community, and the group will grow through your dialogue. Challenge each person to bring a question, a new thought, or a conviction to wrestle with each time you meet.

All book excerpts and articles used by permission.

Editor:
Tim Willard

Contributing Editor:
Jason Haynes

Creative Direction and Design:

FiveStone, Buford, Georgia
www.fivestone.com.

SPECIAL THANKS TO:

Christine, Lyric and Brielle Willard, Jason Locy, Brad Lomenick, Donna Pennell, Jason Haynes, Craig Canfield, Pato Juárez, Teresa Cunningham, Shelley Moore, Ken Coleman, The Mad Hatter, Tony Stark, and all our contributors.

For more information on the Catalyst Conference or to order additional copies of *The Thin Line*, call 888.334.6569 or visit **catalystspace.com.**

ISBN-10: 0-9821354-9-1
ISBN-13: 978-0-9821354-9-5

Printed in the United States of America.
Copyright ©2010 by Catalyst

THE TENSION OF NO

BY ANDY STANLEY

We are all familiar with managing a certain amount of tension. Whether working on an organizational team, leading a church, or spearheading a nonprofit, leaders routinely find themselves in the tension of having more to accomplish than hours in the day.

When we read in Acts about the early church, we find the disciples doing everything with no organization and no hierarchy of leadership. All of the new converts believed that Jesus was coming back soon, so they all stayed in Jerusalem. Thousands of people were coming to faith, there was a growing energy, and everyone was worshiping together—but after a while, the people got hungry and attitudes flared. The disciples had to figure out how to feed all those people—those who were from Jerusalem and those who were from out of town. The first challenge of the local church led to a simple idea and, consequently, some remarkable things happened.

"In those days when the number of disciples was increasing, the Grecian Jews among them complained against the Hebraic Jews because their widows were being overlooked in the daily distribution of food." (Acts 6:1 NIV)

Think about the humor in this. The apostles were actually doing food service! They were teaching and telling about the resurrection and passing out food. They were doing everything.

"So the Twelve gathered all the disciples together and said, 'It would not be *right* for us to neglect the ministry of the Word of God in order to wait on tables." (Acts 6:2)

Now think of how arrogant this must have sounded. Essentially they're saying, "Look, we're *the* guys. We were with Jesus. All those stories you've heard, we were there. We've got a lot going on. We're very busy. But teaching the Word is important, and so is making sure everybody gets fed. But we can't do both. It would be wrong for us to wait on tables and serve the widows and orphans. It would be wrong for us to do that *if* we neglect the thing that we are *uniquely positioned to do*: to tell the story of the gospel. So we are going to find somebody else to serve the widows."

This is an emotionally charged issue—widows and food. And the apostles, in the moment of all of that drama and chaos in Jerusalem, realized they had to play to their strengths and delegate the things they shouldn't be doing.

YOU NEED ME TO SAY *NO*

Every Sunday, I do two morning services and an evening service. And almost every Sunday, someone comes up to me and says: "Andy, can I meet with you?" to which I reply, *No.* Then they say, "Can I get on your calendar?" and I say, *No.* "Hey, could we have lunch?" *No.* I have learned to say *no.*

What I do say is: "Our church is so big that we can help you, but it won't be me." "Well, Andy, I don't mind waiting." *No.*

I've decided that I don't meet with people randomly, and it's not because I don't care. It's because I care so much. And here's what I say, and they never understand:

"The reason you love our church is because I can't meet with you. The reason you love our church is because I play to my strengths. I teach my staff to play to their strengths, and we delegate and hire to play to our weaknesses. Now we have a big staff and church and you love our church because we have all of these resources and programs. The reason you love this church and want to come back is because I *won't* meet with you. It would not be right for me to meet with you and neglect all the other things I'm better at anyway. Can we help you? Absolutely, we can help you. Will it be me? *No.*"

This is not a new concept—my hand is only good at being a hand. My eyes are only good at being eyes. First Corinthians 12:14 says, "The body is not made up of one part, but of many." For some reason, early on in ministry, it's natural and necessary to do everything because we want to set the standard. But the sooner we get into our sweet spots of leadership, the sooner our churches or our ministries will flourish, and the more opportunity we will create for other people.

AS YOU NARROW YOUR FOCUS, YOU CREATE MORE OPPORTUNITY FOR OTHER PEOPLE.

CREATING SPACE

So, when the apostles realized that they couldn't do everything that needed to be done, they called all of the disciples together and made this proposal:

"Brothers, choose seven men from among you who are known to be full of the Spirit and wisdom. We will turn this responsibility over to them and will give our attention to prayer and to the ministry of the Word.

This proposal pleased the whole group. They chose Stephen, a man full of faith and the Holy Spirit; also Philip, Procorus, Nicanor, Timon, Parmenas, and Nicolas from Antioch, a convert to Judaism. They presented these men to the apostles, who prayed and laid their hands on them. So the word of God spread. The number of disciples in Jerusalem increased rapidly, and a large number of priests became obedient to the faith." (Acts 6:3-7)

The church grew. The apostles did fewer things and accomplished more. They leaned into what they were uniquely gifted and called to do, and they created space for other people to do the things they weren't doing a very good job at.

This leadership principle allows those of us in ministry to establish and maintain a sustainable pace. Corporately, we end up with organizations that reflect our strengths, not our weaknesses.

CONCENTRATION, ELIMINATION

Here are some questions to help you figure out your sweet spot.

→ What do you do that seems effortless to you, but is a daunting task to others?
→ In what areas do people consider you the go-to person?
→ What facets of your job energize you?
→ What do you wish you could stop doing?
→ What organizations or environments are you drawn to?
→ What environments do you absolutely try to avoid?
→ Discovery project: Take some time and develop the ideal job description for your current job or ministry.

In a letter to seminary alumni, Howard Hendricks wrote: "If anything has kept me on track all these years, it is being skewered to this principle of central focus. There are many things I can do, but I must narrow it down to the one thing I must do. The secret to concentration is elimination. Only do what only you can do because the less you do the more you accomplish."

God has called you, equipped you, and positioned you to do a few things alongside a lot of people. The sooner you get there, the more replenished you'll be in ministry, the longer you'll stay in ministry, the better example you'll be to the people in ministry around you, and the more you will enjoy this incredible thing that God has given us called the local church. **C**

FROM THE EDITORS

Without tension life can fall into the mundane and uninteresting. If movies had no tension or conflict, we would find ourselves bored. Not only does tension make life riveting, it makes us, as people, dynamic. Daily we throw ourselves into endeavors that push and pull our beliefs and cultural sensibilities. Though tension proves tricky at times, it can be good.

This year we wanted to look at that thin line between the good and the bad, the comfortable and uncomfortable in Christian leadership. Sometimes we fall into the trap of thinking that one approach to leadership or to solving a problem is better simply because it is the opposite of what is being done. But more often than not, a both-and scenario is needed.

Take, for example, John Piper's article titled "Seek It Like Silver." **Dr. Piper** describes how seminary and higher education actually ignited his passion for God and His Word. The life of the mind often receives a mixed bag in Christian circles; some err on anti-intellectualism while others lean too heavily on academics. But what about a both-and approach? What about living in the tension of studying to show yourself approved and your faith expressing itself in active sacrificial love?

Too often, however, this in-between place of tension within leadership proves to be too challenging. Either we back down from the inherent risk or we realize there is a market for just doing the opposite of something.

In dealing with tension, we need to be OK with how it shapes us and where it leads us.

Other topics emerge as well. Discover **Francis Chan's** challenging view on "calling" and eavesdrop on **Brian and Mandy Miller** as they share their thoughts on leading worship in a celebrity-driven culture. **Eugene Cho** pokes our pocketbooks as he tells how he deals with the tension of living in affluence while so many in the world struggle through deep poverty.

Some new faces found their way into our pages this year as well. The First Response Team of America's **Tad Agoglia** explains how fear factors into leadership—a healthy tension that all leaders must face. Tad's pioneering efforts as a natural disaster first responder continue to show the world the power of service and compassion. We also hear from **Kay Warren** who gives us a soaring challenge regarding adoption.

As usual, we tried to remain simple, beautiful, timely, timeless, and deep. As you peruse the content, keep in mind that our goal is to expose you to ideas, causes, and expressions that speak into your current leadership context. And, in quintessential Catalyst fashion, we accomplish this by selecting features and articles that will challenge and encourage you and your team to grow. So, as you tiptoe across the thin line of leadership, remember that balance is not achieved in a vacuum. It is, rather, the culmination of constant tension.

CONTENTS

FEATURES

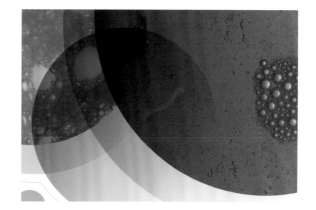

GUARDIANS OF
THE UNGUARDED

BY KAY WARREN

"Who will take care of my children when I die?" she asked in a whisper. "No one will want them because they know I am dying of AIDS." Flora's tears flowed, her face a mixture of anguish and fear. She was the first dying mother I had ever encountered and I had no answers for her; I was nearly mute in the presence of her suffering. My assurances that I would pray for her and her children were woefully inadequate. How could my words of intercession be enough to cover the needs of her soon-to-be-orphaned young children?

Her face, her heartrending question, and the certainty that Flora is no longer here haunts me seven years later. What has happened to her precious babies? Did a kind relative open her home to them? Was a neighbor brave enough to overcome the stigma surrounding HIV and AIDS to welcome these little ones? Did a family in their church listen to the Holy Spirit's promptings and make space at their table for three more hungry mouths? Or are those three children growing up in an institution—an orphanage—that will keep their bodies alive but give them no long-term hope for a normal life? Or even worse: Are they on the unforgiving streets of Maputo, Mozambique, scrounging out an existence? Or worst of all: Did their status as vulnerable orphans lead to an untimely death?

While most of us give very little thought to the one 143 million orphans in the world, *God is passionately con-*

GOD ADOPTED EACH OF US WHEN WE WERE SPIRITUAL ORPHANS, WITHOUT A HOME, A FAMILY, A FATHER. WE WERE VULNERABLE, UNABLE TO EARN OUR WAY INTO HIS FAMILY, AND HAD NOTHING GOING FOR US.

cerned for them. The fact that a child is orphaned due to AIDS every fourteen seconds rips at His heart. The reality that twenty-five percent of the population of Nigeria are orphans grieves Him. The status of Flora's three children is on His mind every day.

In Proverbs 23:10-11 (NLT), God reveals Himself as a powerful guardian for orphans and vulnerable children: "Don't cheat your neighbor by moving the ancient boundary markers; don't take the land of defenseless orphans. For their Redeemer is strong; he himself will bring their charges against you."

In this passage, God uses the example of stealing land from an orphan to reveal how He feels about them. To steal land from a neighbor is obviously wrong, but to take land from a fatherless child is reprehensible in God's eyes! As their powerful guardian, it makes Him furious! Other translations call Him their advocate, their redeemer, their champion, their savior, their deliverer, the All-Powerful God. More than Super Man or Iron Man, they have GOD as their guardian and He will "take up their cause *against you.*"

Don't be fooled by the nice language. God is sending out a warning: He's going to do some serious butt-kicking to anyone who takes advantage of, hurts, manipulates, steals from, exploits, terrorizes, wounds, or in any way hurts vulnerable children. They are under His special protection. He calls Himself the Father to the Fatherless (Ps. 68:5) and He will avenge any wrong done to them. You do NOT want to be on the wrong side of God when it comes to orphans—He is fanatical in His passion and love for them!

So much so that how we treat orphans and widows is a litmus test of our spiritual life and our love for God.

James 1:27 says, "*Pure and lasting religion* in the sight of God our Father means that *we must care* for orphans and widows in their troubles, and refuse to let the world corrupt us."

It's not an option, folks. Caring for orphans and vulnerable children is not just for a few people; this is not a matter of economics or spiritual gifts or personal interests. This is not for some of us, but for ALL of us. Having a heart that is tender toward children without a family is a test of our love for God. If we say we love God but do nothing on behalf of the world's vulnerable children, we're kidding ourselves; we're ignorant and misinformed. You simply cannot love God without developing a passion for orphans.

Scripture also teaches that what God has done for us spiritually, He desires for us to do physically. God adopted each of us when we were spiritual orphans, without a home, a family, a father. We were vulnerable, unable to earn our way into His family, and had nothing going for us. But, because of His unbelievable, amazing mercy and grace, we are now a part of His forever family, equal heirs with our older brother, Jesus. We have been adopted; we know the joy of belonging. From grateful hearts, we must now look at our vulnerable little brothers and sisters and seek a home and a family for them.

Russell Moore says, "Adoption is not just about couples who want children—or who want more children. Adoption is about an entire culture within our churches, a culture that sees adoption as part of our Great Commission mandate and as a sign of the gospel itself."

Not everyone should adopt, but more should than do. Every family should at least ask the question, "God, do You want our family to foster or adopt a child?" How do you know the answer unless you've asked the question?

143 million children—perhaps Flora's three are among them—are waiting for us who name the name of Jesus to take them home. ◼

RAGAMUFFINOLOGY
AN INTERVIEW WITH CARLOS WHITTAKER

Catalyst: On your blog you state that you live "to ignite a movement of authenticity among all generations of Christians that morphs the face of the evangelical church into a place of being real with yourself, others, and God." Tell us how the pursuit of authenticity became so personal to you.

Whittaker: I started going to a church called Sandals Church in Riverside, CA when it was in its infancy. Sandals Church was all about being real with yourself, others, and God. When I first heard that vision statement, I honestly didn't know what it meant. Naturally I assumed, "Of course I'm real with myself, with others, and with God."

But the longer I was there and the longer I started to see Pastor Matt Brown live this out, the more personal it became to me. I began to see how important it was to model authenticity in my life. I was bathed in that truth for ten years at Sandals Church—that's where my journey began and how it became so personal to me.

Catalyst: Can you define "authenticity" for us?

Whittaker: I think in defining what authenticity is it's also helpful to look at what authenticity does *not* mean. Authenticity does *not* mean being rude to people. So many people believe that being authentic gives them a license to just go around giving people an unfiltered piece of their mind. That is *not* authenticity.

Authenticity is about recognizing your own faults, recognizing your own "gifting," and embracing those things in yourself. It's not only about spitting out all your faults for the world to see, but also bringing it back full circle and celebrating the gifts that God gave you. So ask forgiveness when you blow it, but realize that authenticity is when the good, the bad, and sometimes ugly are visible to the world. That's when growth can occur, for His name's sake.

Catalyst: Do you ever feel a tension between being innovative/creative and being authentic? What are some pitfalls the church much watch out for in pursuing innovation?

Whittaker: I do sometimes feel the tension between being innovative and creative and being authentic because so many times creatives have a tendency to stretch the truth. We need to be innovative for the sake of the church and the sake of the gospel, not innovative for the sake of innovation.

We can decide to be innovative for the purpose of "this Sunday's sermon" or "this week's series," but I don't believe that is true innovation unless there is a much bigger picture involved. Without that greater purpose, without the "why," we stop creating and start manufacturing. Authenticity is lost when our goals are self-centered and it is won back when our goals are Christ-centered.

The word *innovate* is thrown around in churches these days to feel hip and relevant. If our purpose is "hipness" or "cool" then we start getting lost in it all. Innovation does not mean *cool*. Innovation means creating something new. When we're trying to package "hip" and "cool" we are no longer creating environments for people to experience God; we're manufacturing them, and when that happens we lose our authenticity.

Catalyst: As a guy who has created a large tribe using social media what would you say to someone who is skeptical of the kind of community created by social media?

Whittaker: I've got a blog called Ragamuffinsoul.com. Thousands of readers come by every day, and over 17,000+ people follow me on Twitter. But do these people know who I am, truly? The answer is no. They know who I want them to know. They know the Carlos Whittaker I create.

I try to create an authentic experience of who I am. Is that always completely feasible and possible? No. Here's the deal, so many people give social media and people whose lives are built on social media a hard time because they're connecting with people sitting on the other side of a 17" LCD screen. But the people that are sitting on the other side of that screen are *actual* people.

For example, right now my family and I are driving across country. Last night I stayed at a friend's house in Oklahoma City with my family of five. I met these friends completely online, and tonight we'll stay in another city with another family my wife met through her blog.

Are we going to become best friends staying with them one night? No. But the truth is while people criticize the computer screen, we know that there are real people sitting behind those screens.

So, as far as people being skeptical of social media? It works. Another example is when my record came out last year. I was a brand new artist on Integrity (music label). I have not toured a day in my life. But I built a tribe that allowed my album to go #1 on iTunes, strictly from the community and relationships built online. So it is feasible, it is possible, and it is also real.

Catalyst: As a worship leader how do you wrestle with the tension of being both a performer and someone whose main purpose is directing others' worship to God?

Whittaker: I'm a worship leader, plain and simple. Live on stage, trying to connect people and shrink the gap between the crowd. It is a struggle for me, because I'm trying to sell records. Here I am as a worship leader saying that the name above all names is Jesus Christ. There is a tension, as I put my name out there because I've got to sell records. I've got to feed my family, but I've got to lift Jesus' name up above mine.

Hopefully, people know that if the worship leader is truly authentic that they have a ministry and need to support their family, but at the same time their ultimate goal is to make famous the name of Jesus. And that is a dance that I think worship leaders and Christian artists are going to have to dance for a long time. ◼

A DIVINE IDENTITY
AN INTERVIEW WITH BRIAN AND MANDY MILLER

Mandy and Brian Miller currently lead worship on various occasions in three different churches in Atlanta: The Vine Community Church (small church plant), North Point Buckhead, and Browns Bridge—both of which are Northpoint satellite campuses. They've also led worship for events like Catalyst and Youth Specialties. Before moving to Atlanta, Brian and Mandy started a college group in Fenton, Michigan, where they served as the worship leaders. Their experience with different venues gives them a unique perspective on the heart of worship leading.

Catalyst: Talk about the tension between leading worship in an environment and culture that's highly produced as opposed to not produced. How does the type of venue affect you?

Mandy: Well, I think that there is always going to be a tension when you're doing something where you can receive the praise of man, while your goal is to be ministering to God.

Personally, I think it helps me to be in venues where this tension forces me to lean into God and to listen to what He's saying to me. When I get off of that stage the only thing that really matters is how He feels about me. So, being in those types of venues tends to intensify the tension because you've got the lights, the stage, amazing sound, and you've got all the people there. I think it can exacerbate the longing for man's approval and the longing to be known.

As long as you are honest with it and bring it before the Lord and say, "Alright God, I want to look into the mirror of Your face every day and ask how You feel about me, and am I following You? Am I open to You? Because all of the rest of this stuff doesn't really matter." In some ways it's been good for me because it's forced me to wrestle with these questions: "Who am I?" "Is being a worship leader my identity?"

At the end I am called to minister to God. I'm not even called, ultimately, to minister to man; I'm called to stand before Him, and to sing my heart out to Him about how much I love Him. God's the one who ministers to *us*. He flows through people, but it's Him doing it.

Catalyst: Some people love the big production worship services and others don't. How does the high production aspect of worship help or hinder a worship service? How does it impact the congregation?

Brian: I think there's a tension as people are always looking for physical leadership. Leadership is essential, because when we gather more than a few people in a room you need leadership, you need direction and structure. I think one of the tensions is while we want physical leadership, we are also completely prone to make golden calves. As Richard Keyes says, our hearts are "idol factories." We're so prone to make idols out of things, so at the same moment that we want somebody to lead us, there's also the danger that we can make an idol out of that person.

I think this is a tension to be managed and I don't know if the tension can be resolved, because if you go superhigh on production, you've got this tension, but if you go "unplugged" you've still got the tension of making an idol out of physical leadership. Either way I think the issue is in the heart, and we need to address that, as worship leaders.

We also have to prayerfully consider the technology we're using and the ways we're using it. We rarely discuss technology. We just assume that, "Oh, this is what's working," or "This is what everyone else is doing." So we do it, as opposed to having thoughtful conversations about it. Let's at least grapple with these questions and come to conclusions that we have peace about.

Catalyst: Talk about success in the "worship leader" realm. Is there such a thing?

Brian: Unfortunately, success often gets equated with size. "I'm not as successful as so-and-so because they're on the stage or at this level of ministry." But that misses the mark. We need to pursue that which God has given us to do with our whole heart—whether that's a ministry of five, twenty-five, or twenty-five hundred.

Mandy: Self-evaluation is key: "Am I viewing my success or my identity through the eyes of man or God?" God has specifically told me, "Mandy, I'm not calling you to be a rock star, I'm calling you to be My child. That's your identity. I'm not calling you to the masses. I'm calling you to the helpless and the hopeless, the people who are in need. That's where I'm drawing you because that's where My heart is." Once your heart starts following after the masses just for the masses' sake, something is wrong there.

Catalyst: What are some safeguards you guys implement and that other worship leaders can use to keep their egos and spiritual lives in check?

Brian: I think that we need to be grounded in community. By that I mean we need to be involved in vibrant relationships where people can know the real us. We need people in our lives with whom we can take off our masks, where we can be honest and confess our sins to one another, pray for one another. People who know the real you have a way of humbling you while at the same time encouraging you.

Mandy: Listening to the Holy Spirit and what He's saying to you is vital. He may call you to do things that are not the norm. But He knows the specific purpose He has called you to. When we begin listening to others more than to God, we lose our boldness and become afraid to step out and do things that maybe go against the flow. He's the one we're worshiping so we need to go to Him and ask Him what He wants. He knows us. C

THE TROUBLE WITH THE TWO E'S

BY JONATHAN ACUFF

Sometimes I fear we are a generation of people doing things we don't love.

I say this because inevitably when I meet new people they use the "I'm, but" approach to life.

"I'm an accountant, but I want to be an artist."

"I'm a teacher, but I want to be an abolitionist."

"I'm a web developer, but I want to be a youth minister."

We're caught in the endless tension between doing what we have to do—pay the bills, be responsible, make good on college degrees, and what we want to do—feel alive, feel necessary, be part of something bigger than ourselves.

Usually what happens is that we unknowingly end up making a choice between one of the two E's. We either pursue what we are called to and become *Engaged*. Or we stagnate and become *Entitled*. We make that "leap of faith" necessary for any adventure and find ourselves engaged with something wild and beautiful and true. Or we grumble and complain and find ourselves frustrated because we're entitled to so much more.

This was my struggle while writing the book Stuff Christians Like as I worked in an IT department. I liked my job. I really enjoyed that company, but it was honestly hard to get up at five in the morning and write as hard as I could on the book before going in for an eight-hour workday.

The temptation was to give in to the sense of entitlement. I deserved to write a book. Since I was in the third grade, that was my goal, so why wasn't it happening? Didn't God see me? Didn't he know what was possible? Where were my eagle wings to soar out of my cubicle and into the wide-open magical land of book writing, where publishing deals galloped like unicorns?

Have you ever felt that way? Has God ever felt too slow or too impersonal or too disengaged from your heart's desire for something else? A different job, a different city, a different movement? I have, and in those moments it's easy to ball up your fists and get entitled.

What does that look like?
How do you know if you're there?

HERE ARE SOME SIGNS:

Entitled people are always exhausted by their dream. *Engaged* people are refreshed and energized. Sure, they might be tired from the hard work but they are not drained in a negative way.

Entitled people repel friends the more they talk about their dream because it is laced with disappointment. *Engaged* people attract people because the joy of their dream is infectious.

Entitled people believe in the myth of "overnight success." *Engaged* people know that working at what they dream about is part of the reward of the experience.

Entitled people wait for major life changes to get started. They make excuses like, "If I had more time I would be able to write this book!" *Engaged* people start right where they are and realize there's no "perfect time" to pursue a dream.

Entitled people see the success of others as a personal insult. *Engaged* people celebrate when someone else wins.

HAVE YOU EVER FELT THAT WAY? HAS GOD EVER FELT TOO SLOW OR TOO IMPERSONAL OR TOO DISENGAGED FROM YOUR HEART'S DESIRE FOR SOMETHING ELSE? A DIFFERENT JOB, A DIFFERENT CITY, A DIFFERENT MOVMENT? I HAVE, AND IN THOSE MOMENTS IT'S EASY TO BALL UP YOUR FISTS AND GET ENTITLED.

There are countless other signs, but those are the ones I have seen in my own life. Writing my site (www.stuffchristianslike.net) used to wear me out because I was manically developing it. It was an obsession, not a passion. I repelled my friends by selfishly over-talking about the site. I was so frustrated by other bloggers who had book deals because I didn't have one yet and felt like I deserved my "overnight moment."

I was entitled and it just about emptied me.

Don't let the tension between the two E's get you too. Lean toward being engaged. Aim for engaged. Cling to engaged. It's harder than entitled sometimes, being a jerk is easy, but I promise you that engaged is worth it.

Let's not be a generation of people doing things we don't love. ■

LOVE, LIGHT & MELODY

A NEW SONG

Last year we came across an organization called Love, Light & Melody. Musician Brad Corrigan started LL&M after he was invited to play a benefit concert and youth rally in Managua, Nicaragua. The trip exposed him to a country that reels from stark and intense social extremes: elite upper-class and extreme poverty. One of the by-products of this social imbalance is the city trash dump. The mountain of trash is home to hundreds of people who depend on the garbage for their livelihood, food and shelter.

After several visits to the dump, Brad met the most unlikely and beautiful little girl, Ileana. She introduced him to her family and a vibrant community living in the shadows of the forgotten and discarded. Inspired by these newfound friends, Love Light & Melody was officially formed in 2007 to meet the educational, health, and vocational needs of this trash dump community.

"When you walk with someone you're saying to them, 'I am with you.' We can walk in hell and not have fear." This powerful statement guides the vision for LL&M. Each year, the organization invites friends, family, and college students to join them for Dia de Luz to celebrate a profound love conquering hate, a beautiful light overcoming darkness, and a resounding melody breaking silence.

Brad's passion to serve this small and forgotten community has blossomed into a team given to his vision. LL&M reminds us that even in the darkest hour, there is always Light. C

To find out how you can help LL&M use the arts to rebuild, restore and bring healing to communities ravaged by extreme poverty visit their website at: www.lovelightandmelody.org

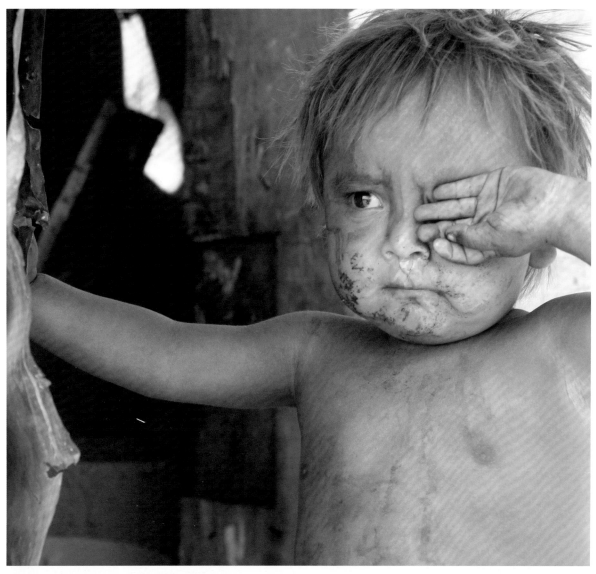

COLLECTIVE THINKING

BY REGGIE JOINER

Collective thinking requires the kind of tension that leads to healthy debate.

A disclaimer: The following statements do not necessarily reflect my opinions, even though I wrote them. I like to write out loud before I have convinced myself of what I think. It may seem dangerous, but for me it is a necessary process and part of what we're talking about when we introduce the idea of positive tension.

Our staff frequently puts controversial ideas on a creative board to spark conversation. Why? Because we have a passion to reach the next generation and we believe the right amount of tension leads to meaningful dialogue, strong debate, and hard-fought decisions. The best ideas and solutions are a result of difficult conversations where we express differing opinions.

I encourage you to dialogue with your team about the following kinds of topics. Create your own statements so you can invite each other into the kind of debate that will keep you learning as an organization. Remember, the point of the exercise is to help you create a healthy tension that will stretch everyone on your team. Here are a few statements to get you started:

WE DON'T NEED TO START ANY MORE CHURCHES

Or at least we don't need to start another church like the church that already exists down the road. What if we decided to only start churches for people who are not already going to church? Admit it: most start-up churches are designed for people who already attend. Should our goal be to create the same style of church that already exists to reach the people who are already attending another church that it's already like? Maybe we should create a church that is different enough to present an alternative for those who can't find a church. So if you are going to start a church, consider doing something that's not being done.

PARENTS AREN'T ENOUGH

Yes, parents have the potential to influence their children more than anyone else. But it is just as true that parents are not the only adult influence kids need. As children move toward the independence of their teenage years, they need affirmation from someone besides their parents. Young people who have consistent adult influences other than their own parents stand a better chance of having a dynamic and mobilized faith.

So, while we need to organize our churches so that we invite parents to become more intentional about engaging in the moral and spiritual formation of their own children, we also need to establish a strategy that develops other adults as mentors and coaches in the lives of kids and teenagers.

ABSTINENCE IS NOT THE MOST IMPORTANT THING WE CAN TEACH TEENAGERS ABOUT SEX

We work hard to convince teenagers that abstinence before marriage will yield great sex life after they say, "I do." So those who wait to have sex have some pretty high expectations. What if sexual fulfillment has less to do with abstinence and more to do with something else? Am I suggesting that abstinence isn't important? No. As the father of three daughters, let me restate that again just in case you missed it. *It is important to teach teenagers the value of abstinence!* But what if abstinence is not the only essential concept we need to teach?

Is it dangerous to teach that abstinence is the answer to everything? Many couples who struggle with issues in the bedroom were "technical virgins" before they got married. Abstinence does not replace the need to understand true intimacy and develop a proper respect for the opposite gender.

TEENAGERS ARE NOT MORE IMPORTANT THAN THOSE WHO ARE COLLEGE-AGE

For over forty years the trend of 18 to 25-year-olds leaving church continues to rise. While college students continue to fade out of the picture, denominations and churches are getting older. Most church leaders don't have a plan to stop the trend. Most churches think of college students as temporary, transient, and non-tithing.

Too many of us have programmed a finish line for young people at twelfth grade. We push our seniors out the door, breathe a sigh of relief, and let them disappear for a few years. We assume they will spend the next several years building their faith, starting a career, getting married, and showing back up at our churches when they are more "complete." So we let them go.

But what if we have drawn the wrong finish line? What if the relational connection is more important in college than it ever was in high school? They're making some of the most important decisions they'll ever make. Don't we want to find a way to be involved in influencing those decisions?

CONSIDER THIS

Here are a few other statements we would suggest for your team to think about. I hesitate to just throw them out there without any explanation, but I will anyway, just to keep things tense:

→ Stop doing something that works so something else can work better.
→ Sometimes discipleship is more about serving than it is about Bible study.
→ There is no ideal picture in the Bible of what a family should look like.
→ Every Christian is not a Republican. Every Christian is not a Democrat. Or either.
→ What you don't teach as a leader can be as important as what you do teach.
→ Jesus didn't preach very many expository messages.

Remember, I am not asking you to agree or disagree. Just establish a habit of crafting statements that create positive tension. Learn to value healthy debate and think collectively. **C**

COMMUNITY FOR THE AGELESS
VALUING THE WISDOM OF THOSE MORE (AND LESS) EXPERIENCED

BY MIKE SARES

Dr. James Means of Denver Seminary was my mentor during the time I was asked to resign from a Presbyterian church and then during the time I was deciding what to do next. He was more than a couple of decades older than me. We used to meet at a bagel shop and discuss what was going on in my life. At one point, I had a couple of offers from large churches to come and pastor their single adult ministries. I told him about those possibilities, and then I shared with Dr. Means my belief that God was up to something with the skaters and punks with whom I'd been working in the Capitol Hill District of Denver. But now, sadly, I would have to leave them.

Dr. Means thought for a while and then opened up. He had been called to a small church in the suburbs of Denver some forty years before; had he not accepted the position it would have undoubtedly gone to someone else. The church would have chosen another pastor who preached the gospel, he said, and because of the church's location and the growth of the population of Denver at that time, the church would have surely grown even as it had under his guidance. And then he said, "Maybe it would have done better with someone else than with me."

He went on to say that twenty years ago, when the seminary asked him to become its professor of pastoral ministries, he accepted the job—but had he not accepted the position, the seminary would have chosen someone else. And then quite humbly he added, "Perhaps they would have chosen someone better qualified than me."

Then he shifted in his chair, lowered his voice, and said, "But you know Mike, when I go to Africa and teach pastoral students in a grass-roofed hut or when I'm with the medical missions team there and am inoculating African babies against disease—I know that when I'm on the plane returning to the United States that no one is going back to take my place."

Then he stopped talking and looked at me.

There was a long, awkward silence. I don't know if you've ever experienced those kind of long pauses where the first one to speak loses, but I understood exactly what he was saying. If I did not accept the mega-church positions that I was being offered, then undoubtedly someone else would come along and fill those roles. But if I did not go and minister to those who were the "left out" in the Capitol Hill District, then no one else was going to take my place.

A PAIN IN THE BUTT

Sitting in the bagel shop with Dr. Means, this professor was gently challenging me to risk everything for the sake of following Christ. I had been looking for the highest paying job within the will of God. I had a wife and four children. I had a mortgage to pay. And there was no way a bunch of skater-punks was going to help with that.

Godly counsel from a trusted, older mentor is often a pain in the butt.

Eventually, with the help of people a couple of decades younger than me (and a bunch of people my age to foot the bill), Scum of the Earth Church was launched. We opened worship services gathered in the converted living room of an old house in Capitol Hill. The place had been turned into a drop-in coffee house for street kids, but it still looked more like somebody's home than a Starbucks.

There were, maybe, two dozen people in attendance. Most sat on the hard wooden floor, a few sat on the couch or on the kitchen counter. Songs were being led by a guy and a girl sitting cross-legged on the floor, playing guitars cradled in their laps. There was an overhead projector shining its distended rectangle of light on an old screen that had been repaired with some wire. I felt like I was

suddenly back in the 1970s somewhere, caught up in the tide of the Jesus Movement. It was grand.

My illusions of nostalgia were shattered when I met with Reese Roper, my young co-pastor, the next week to debrief.

"What happened to you?" he asked.

"What are you talking about?"

"Your sermon didn't sound like you at all. It sounded like you were trying to impress someone at my mom's church," he explained.

"What? I don't get it." I was clueless.

"Why don't you just talk to us like you talk to me over coffee? You need to sound like yourself. We like Mike. I don't know who you were trying to be."

HE WAS CALLING ME BACK TO SOMETHING I SHOULD HAVE KNOWN.

I felt like I had been frozen stiff and was beginning to thaw. By the time Scum of the Earth began I was already 46 years old. There was no way I was going to try to look and speak like I was in my twenties. Reese wasn't asking me to change the way I looked. He was calling me back to something I should have known.

Godly counsel from a trusted, younger subordinate is often a bigger pain in the butt.

It is natural to look to those who are older for wisdom and accountability. But we must not resist humbling ourselves to accept that same kind of severe blessing from those younger, for the Spirit of the Living God resides in them, too. The truth be told, I never wanted the name Scum of the Earth for our attempt to do church. Perhaps I was afraid of it. Maybe I was too insecure to lead a church with a name like that. But I "gave in" to those I led, and it was the best decision I never made. God's community is ageless. **C**

YOU'RE A RACIST,
YOU KNOW

BY TIMOTHY KELLER

Although I had grown up going to church, Christianity began to lose its appeal to me when I was in college. One reason for my difficulty was the disconnect between my secular friends who supported the Civil Rights Movement, and the orthodox Christian believers who thought that Martin Luther King, Jr., was a threat to society. Why, I wondered, did the nonreligious believe so passionately in equal rights and justice, while the religious people I knew could not have cared less?

A breakthrough came when I discovered a small but thoughtful group of devout Christian believers who were integrating their faith with every kind of justice in society. At first I merely imported my views on racial justice from my college years and added them onto the theology I was learning as a Christian. I didn't see what later I came to realize, that in fact the Bible is the very basis for justice. I learned that the creation account in Genesis was the origin for the idea of human rights in the West[1] and that biblical prophetic literature rang with calls for justice.

Years afterward I discovered that the Civil Rights Movement of the 1950s and '60s I so admired was grounded much more in the African-American church's Christian views of sin and salvation than in secularism.[2] When I went to seminary to prepare for the ministry, I met an

African-American student, Elward Ellis, who befriended both my future wife, Kathy Kristy, and me. He gave us gracious but bare–knuckled mentoring about the realities of injustice in American culture.

"You're a racist, you know," he once said at our kitchen table.

"Oh, you don't mean to be, and you don't want to be, but you are. You can't really help it." He said, for example, "When black people do things in a certain way, you say, 'Well, that's your culture.' But when white people do things in a certain way, you say, 'That's just the right way to do things.' You don't realize you really have a culture. You are blind to how many of your beliefs and practices are cultural."

We began to see how, in so many ways, we made our cultural biases into moral principles and then judged people of other races as being inferior. His case was so strong and fair that, to our surprise, we agreed with him.

While I was in my first pastorate in Hopewell, Virginia, I decided to enroll in a doctor of ministry program, and my project (the "thesis" of the course) was on training deacons. In Presbyterian church organization, there are two sets of lay (nonprofessional) officers—elders and deacons. Deacons had historically been designated to work with the poor and needy in the community, but over the years this legacy had been lost, and instead they had evolved into janitors and treasurers. My program advisor challenged me to study the history of the office and to develop ways to help Presbyterian churches recover this lost aspect of their congregational life.

I took the assignment and it was a transformative process for me. I went to the social work department of a nearby university, got the full reading list for their foundational courses, and devoured all the books. I did historical research on how church deacons served as the first public social service structure in European cities such as Geneva, Amsterdam, and Glasgow. I devised courses of skill-training for deacons and wrote material to help church leaders get a vision not only for the "word" ministry of preaching and teaching, but also for "deed" ministry, serving people with material and economic needs.[3]

After my pastorate in Virginia, I went to teach at Westminster Seminary in Philadelphia. In my department were four faculty members who lived in the inner city and taught urban ministry. Each week I would go to the department meeting a bit early and have fifteen minutes or so alone talking with the chairman, Harvie Conn. Harvie was passionately committed to living and working in the city, and he was keenly aware of the systemic injustice in our society. As I look back on those times, I realize I was learning far more from him than at the time I thought I was. I read his little book *Evangelism: Doing Justice and Preaching Grace*[4] twenty–five years ago and its themes sank deep into my thinking about God and the church.

Inspired by Harvie's teaching and by all the experiences I had in urban churches in Philadelphia during the 1980s, I answered an invitation to move to the middle of New York City in 1989 and begin a new congregation, Redeemer Presbyterian Church.

ON GRACE AND BEING JUST

There are many great differences between the small southern town of Hopewell, Virginia, and the giant metropolis of New York. But there was one thing that was exactly the same. To my surprise, there is a direct relationship between a person's grasp and experience of God's grace, and his or her heart for justice and the poor. In both settings, as I preached the classic message that God does not give us justice but saves us by free grace, I discovered that those most affected by the message became the most sensitive to the social inequities around them.

One man in my church in Hopewell, Easley Shelton, went through a profound transformation. He moved out of a sterile, moralistic understanding of life and began to understand that his salvation was based on the free, unmerited grace of Jesus. It gave him a new warmth, joy, and confidence that everyone could see. But it had another surprising effect. "You know," he said to me one day, "I've been a racist all my life." I was startled, because I had not yet preached to him or to the congregation on that subject. He had put it together for himself. When he lost his Pharisaism, his spiritual self-righteousness, he said, he lost his racism.

Elaine Scarry of Harvard has written a fascinating little book called *On Beauty and Being Just.*[5] Her thesis is that the experience of beauty makes us less self-centered and more open to justice. I have observed over the decades that when people see the beauty of God's grace in Christ, it leads them powerfully toward justice. **C**

THE ADVENTURE OF GOOD
LAND OF A THOUSAND HILLS

When you think of coffee in America certain images pop into your mind: cozy environments, robust brews, hipster music. We love our coffee and we don't mind paying a little bit more for a great cup. But the coffee experience tends to fizzle after the nice branding becomes commonplace and the third-place becomes passe. We come, we buy, and we go about our day sipping expensive coffee drinks that do little more than dent our pocketbooks.

But what if a coffee company offered one of the best cups of java around and even a few nice coffee houses to enjoy music and idle banter with friends? What if a coffee company offered customers a chance to help infuse hope and dignity into a community on another continent? What if every cup of coffee you bought from this company improved this community's economy and helped heal broken relationships? What if buying a cup of coffee did some good?

In 2001 Jonathan Golden, founder of Land of a Thousand Hills (LOTH), recognized a simple and tangible opportunity to make a difference in the reconciliation process of the Rwandan people. The introduction of Specialty Coffee to the healing fields of Rwanda proved to be an uncommon opportunity for once warring countrymen to not only rebuild their homesteads, but to work together toward lasting peace. The initial investment was small: a roaster off of eBay, buying a bean washing station for the Rwandan's to use, and old fashioned commitment to making an excellent product.

Jonathan's idea, birthed out of his doctoral studies at Gordon-Conwell, reflects his passion to bring an alternative to modern-day capitalism. "It's not just about sending money to help poor people," explains Jonathan. "That's a cop-out. It's about making a difference through the work we do. By working with one Rwandan community, we establish trust, inspire hope, and present a common goal that leads, ultimately, to reconciliation. Everyone involved gains something personally and capitalistically."

The idea of reconciliation acts as *the* thread for LOTH. By producing an outstanding product the company continues to encourage the people of Bukonya (the name of the community) to work together. The people, then, move further away from the division that caused so much heartache and toward something they love—a great source of pride. The reconciliation thread attaches a special moral element to the coffee-making process. For LOTH, doing good isn't about handouts or money raising. Doing good is a way *to be*, in work and all of life.

So, when you see Jonathan at events all over the country promoting LOTH, he will tell you to "Drink coffee. Do good." And that's exactly what you do when you buy a bag of their robust brew. You literally *do good*. Because of your purchase, somewhere in Rwanda a farmer gets to keep farming coffee beans, a family gets to provide education for their children, and weak hearts find strength to love again, to live again. ◼

ONE DAY'S WAGES
AN INTERVIEW WITH EUGENE CHO

BY BRAD LOMENICK

Meet Eugene Cho. He turns 40 in 2010. He and his wife have been married fourteen years with three beautiful children. Born in Korea, raised in San Francisco, he now resides in Seattle where he pastors Quest Church, a church of 400 adults. He doesn't have a massive staff. In fact, he and his wife are the staff. His entrepreneurial spirit helped him start a nonprofit café/music venue called Q Café. Eugene would like you to give up one day's wage.

Lomenick: What is One Day's Wages?

Cho: One Day's Wages (ODW) is a new grassroots movement of people, stories, and actions to alleviate extreme global poverty. It promotes awareness, invites simple giving, and supports sustainable relief through partnerships, especially with smaller organizations in developing regions.

We want to inspire people around the world to donate one day's wages and to renew that pledge at some point; or to start campaigns with a cause by donating their birthday, one day of work, or numerous other ideas to the cause of alleviating extreme global poverty.

Our "one day's wages" equals approximately 0.4% of our annual salary. This amount has a dramatic impact on extreme poverty. That's the message that we're trying to convey. We've raised about $300,000 from regular people donating their one day's wages.

But it's not just about those people in South East Asia or Africa; it's also about you and me. Generosity is not just for the purpose of blessing other people, but it's to rescue us from the abyss of our greed.

Lomenick: Why did you start One Day's Wages?

Cho: We all want to make an impact in this world. We're wired that way. For me, I think it began when I went back to Korea and had a conversation with my grandparents. They told stories of how they lived in extreme poverty, and how privileged I am because of God's grace over our lives. So, I began to learn more about extreme poverty, about this disparity in the world between the rich and poor.

Three years ago I went to visit Burma. I had a chance to see the faces behind all of these statistics that I had been memorizing over the years. It hit home. I thought, as a follower of Christ, this didn't compute. I needed to do something.

Lomenick: You and your family have made major sacrifices in your lives. Talk about the "why" behind this decision.

Cho: When I was in Burma, visiting the villages in the jungles, I asked them what some of their challenges were. One of them was education.

So I asked one of the elders in the village, "What's so hard about providing education?" He responded, "Teacher salaries." So I asked, "How much does it cost to provide teacher salaries?" He said, "$40." In my mind, I thought, *it couldn't be per day, maybe per week*. So I asked. He shook his head, "No. Per year."

Even though statistics about poverty are drastic, I felt I could make a difference and inspire people to do the same. When I returned home my wife and I prayed for some time and felt led to give up our yearly salary. I thought it would be easy—we could sell off assets or something. But then we had this thing called the global economic crisis. [laughs]

It was really hard. Honestly, looking back now if I had known how difficult it was going to be, I don't know if I would have done it. I'm thankful for God's grace that He doesn't always reveal what will come before us. So we went through a lot, but it has been great learning how to obey.

I AM IN THE .86 RICHEST PERCENTILE IN THE WORLD. I KNOW THAT WE'RE GOING THROUGH A RECESSION BUT WE NEED TO REMEMBER THAT WE ARE BLESSED.

Lomenick: What did this decision look like financially for you? (You've been very public with this information.)

Cho: Our household salary is $68,000 a year. Here's some context: $68,000 puts me, in terms of the richest people in the world, at number 52,040,162. I am in the .86 richest percentile in the world. I know that we're going through a recession but we need to remember that we are blessed.

Lomenick: How can the Catalyst community make a difference since we're coming from a similar story?

Cho: I think it begins with a personal conviction. Do you really believe that your life is valuable? Do you really believe that God can use you? I don't have a really profound theological answer. It just stems from: do you truly believe that you as a person are valuable? That you are valued in God's eyes and that God has given you gifts and talents, resources and skills, for His glory and kingdom? If you say you don't, I would say in response that's blasphemous. It is contrary to the truth.

I think it's just us saying, "God, who am I? Who do I serve? And what do You want me to do?" **C**

Find out how you can team with Catalyst and One Day's Wages in the fight against poverty: www.onedayswages.org/catalyst

WHY CHRISTIANS MUST REJECT
POP-ENVIRONMENTALISM

BY JONATHAN MERRITT

I had spoken in front of large audiences before, but this was different. This was an assembly of college students, and having recently been a college student myself, I knew that it would be a tougher crowd than *Mystery Science Theater*. A horn bellowed a high note and the band started playing, which signaled the procession. I marched behind the college president, who was robed in his academic regalia, as we entered an arena filled with more than a thousand students and faculty members.

I wondered why they invited me to be the keynote speaker for the school's annual convocation. I had been selected by the college's vice president of admissions because he felt "a young face might connect better with the students" and because my passions and recent work corresponded to their chosen theme for the upcoming school year: "It's Easy Being Green."

The VP told me that each year his staff picks a theme for the school year, which they promote campus-wide. This year they chose environmentalism. To help the students begin the journey down the green path, they provided every student a copy of an environmental book and a green T-shirt with "It's easy being green" printed across the back. Every student would read the book and then listen to me unpack the whole "green

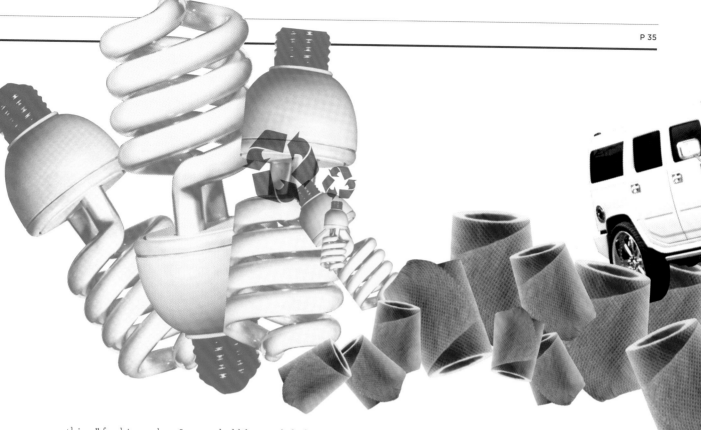

thing" for him or her. It sounded like a solid plan, and I was happy to play a part. I looked forward to seeing the book.

When the book arrived, I had no idea what to expect. The school is a prestigious academic institution, so I assumed the book would be scholarly. I hoped it wouldn't be too thick. It is a Christian college, and I thought the book would perhaps take a juicy, theological angle, which I would love.

I ripped open the package like a seven-year-old opening a gift from Santa. I pulled out a tiny book with a green, embossed cover. The shock must have been evident on my face. With less than 150 pages of text between the covers, the slim volume seemed better suited for a coffee table than a classroom. I was also surprised by the book's content. It had nothing to do with theology. Each chapter concluded with an essay from a celebrity—Justin Timberlake, Cameron Diaz, Will Ferrell, Jennifer Aniston, and Ellen DeGeneres—on how to live green.

Slouching back in my red recliner and staring at the book, I asked myself: "What message is this book sending?" The only answer I came up with frustrated me: "You should 'go green' because it's cool."

THE GREEN TRAIN: ALL ABOARD

Where is America today? America is standing in a checkout lane with a pack of cool-looking, compact fluorescent light bulbs. America is swinging by the neighborhood grocery store to snatch up a couple rolls of unbleached, recycled paper towels. America is not cold because she is wrapped in organic cotton and faux fur. America is not stranded on the side of the road because she is purchasing hybrid vehicles in record numbers. America is not hungry because she has been munching on gourmet organic snacks. America is bragging about these things everywhere from the homeowners' association to church events.

"Clearly, eco-awareness is no longer beardy, worthy, or dull," writes Mimi Spencer of the *UK Guardian*. "In one of the greatest retail revolutions of our times, it's hot. Green is glam. Sustainability is sexy."[1] Green is like the star high school quarterback of cultural movements. What was once reserved for Birkenstock-wearing flower children has hit mainstream culture. Green is the new black. It's trendy, en vogue, and cosmopolitan.

Everything from your neighborhood supermarket to couture fashion has been marked by the fad. An outdoorwear company, Patagonia, produces fleece jackets made from recycled plastic bottles. Diane von Furstenberg,

Oscar de la Renta, Nike, and Levis all offer eco-friendly items. Even Sam's Club now sells jeans and T-shirts made with organic cotton, making Wal-Mart the largest purchaser of organic cotton in the world as of 2006.[2]

Every time I turn on the television, it seems a celebrity is promoting his or her newest environmental pet project. Bono's wife has a line of environmentally responsible designer clothing named Edun ("nude" spelled backwards), Leonardo DiCaprio drives a relatively inexpensive hybrid, Julia Roberts wrapped her twins in eco-friendly diapers and lives in a solar-powered home, and Arnold Schwarzenegger has converted his Hummer to run on hydrogen fuel. Celebs have helped spread environmentalism well beyond the sandalista crowd by helping make it cool, if not sexy. "Have you joined the mainstream on this issue yet?" asks *Fortune* writer Adam Lashinsky in his article "Be Green—Everybody's Doing It."[3]

The message reverberating through culture beckons us to "go green" because we will look better and feel better and fit in, but the movement often feels flimsy and lacking moral foundation.

THE NATURE OF FADS

I never want to run away from anything because it is considered cool or fun by the secular world. I also never want to run toward anything because it is considered cool. Some say the latter tendency is a mistake that many in my own generation have made, which produces faith communities indistinguishable from the rest of culture.

Both cultural separatism and cultural syncretism are unhealthy and unproductive. As a Christian, I want to enjoy many of mainstream culture's gifts and even participate in, contribute to, and shape culture. On my journey to a biblical understanding of creation care, I had to address the green fad. I immediately stumbled upon several problems.

Readers who are older than me may remember the hippie movement that peaked in the 1960s and 1970s. (For some of you, this time might be slightly hazy, but you may still remember parts of it!) Environmentalism was all the rage during these decades, much as it is today. The Clean Air Act was enacted and extended with support from both political parties; pictures of the earth taken by astronauts raised awareness of the earth as a sensitive, life-supporting ecosystem; and tens of thousands of American colleges and schools celebrated Earth Day for the first time.

Environmentalism then went to Washington and into the courts, leaving its grass roots behind. Professionals and lawyers were soon running the movement, and the regular folks were cut out of the process. As political tides changed, corporations became king and environmentalism lost its stylishness in the public consciousness. Popular support waned, and political parties began using the environment as a weapon to beat each other up. Clean air and water became greater problems, and land was clear-cut to make way for cookie-cutter neighborhoods. Today, eco-awareness is making a comeback. Unfortunately, the problems don't go away when the fads do.

Fads come and go, but environmental problems require steady work and constant attention. If we take God's plan to care for creation seriously, we cannot do so because it is trendy. If that's our only motivation, we will find ourselves in dire straits tomorrow when public interest and attention have waned.

A DEEPER GREEN

The biggest reason I reject pop environmentalism is because it cheapens the issue. We have deeper reasons to go green. We serve the Creator of the planet that green living preserves. He created this earth and took the time to tell us His plan for it. The God of this universe has given us the great task of caring for our planet. I like the way Charles Colson addresses this issue in his book *The Body*:

We should be contending for truth in every area of life. Not for power or because we are taken with some trendy cause, but humbly to bring glory to God. For this reason, Christians should be the most ardent ecologists. Not because we would rather save spotted owls than cut down trees whose bark provides lifesaving medicine, but because we are mandated to keep the Garden, to ensure that the beauty and grandeur God has reflected in nature is not despoiled . . . Francis of Assisi should be our role model, not Ted Turner or Ingrid Newkirk.[4]

Why should we be consumed with a "trendy cause" when we have been given a sacred task? I encourage the things mentioned above. Energy-reducing light bulbs, fuel-efficient vehicles, and organic foods are wonderful. The caution is not *what* we are doing, but *why* we are doing it.

When I think, act, respond, and live biblically, I have found people are disarmed. When I am grounded in Scripture, my fellow Christians who view environmentalism as Earth worship, for example, begin to grasp the

"theology of nature" and understand that I can't help but worship the Creator. They also realize that it is impossible to worship the Creator fully without valuing all of His creation.

THE BIGGEST REASON I REJECT POP ENVIRONMENTALISM IS BECAUSE IT CHEAPENS THE ISSUE. WE HAVE DEEPER REASONS TO GO GREEN. WE SERVE THE CREATOR OF THE PLANET THAT GREEN LIVING PRESERVES. HE CREATED THIS EARTH AND TOOK THE TIME TO TELL US HIS PLAN FOR IT.

My speech that day went great, and even the cynical college students loved it—not because I am the best speaker, but because God has given me such illuminating material. Science and statistics are helpful and trends may often serve a purpose, but Scripture is our ultimate guide. When we root ourselves in God's timeless truth, we find a power that can literally restore the world. **C**

THAT NASTY MEGAPHONE

BY JASON YOUNG

Pain touches everyone. Life tends to bombard us with difficult and uncomfortable situations that often leave us lurching through physical and mental pain. We can all point to recent situations that continue to fester as well as the scars from past pains. For some, pain becomes a motivator but for many, pain paralyzes us in fear and doubt and loneliness.

For me, pain has come from a myriad of places. I remember not getting a position at a church that I thought was best for me. I remember leaving a church because a man who attended the church decided he needed to run things, and it quickly became an unhealthy mess. I remember serving under a pastor who struggled to lead anyone. I remember leaving a job too early simply because I was unhappy. I remember struggling through a strained friendship.

These situations hurt me—some deeply—and left me lonely and disappointed. I wanted to quit. I wanted to run away. I'm sure you can tell a story or two, stories that would trump anything I've experienced.

Recently, Craig Groeschel taught me that a leader's constant companion is pain. If this is true, then how can we manage our relationship with pain? It seems that everyone on the planet is always trying to work through some kind of hurt or disappointment. It's hard to just let go of those feelings. They often get the best of us and surface at the most inopportune times.

For me, I visited a counselor (several times). He helped me channel my feelings and provided some timely direction. I would like to say that this fixed it all. But it prompted me to head in another direction; the blame direction. I was often quick to react to my wife and kids during these periods of time. I would find someone to blame instead of being honest and dealing with my pain. I did not always handle pain very well.

After many years, I learned a life-changing truth: pain could be a defining moment, accelerating toward the plan that God wanted me to accomplish. I began to understand that pain was a catalyst, not a hindrance; an opportunity for growth, not an excuse for poor behavior.

But who signs up for pain? Not many people. And even if they do, we might categorize them as crazy. Crazy, however, is not so bad.

It's not that we sign up for pain, it's that we seek for the deeper lesson. We don't allow pain to paint our lifestyle—one marked by bitterness and reactionary practices that end up marring our ministries and vocations.

DO NOT ALLOW PAIN TO RESTRAIN YOU.
THERE IS SO MUCH IN FRONT OF YOU THAT
BECKONS YOUR ATTENTION, YOUR SKILLS,
AND YOUR TIME. TODAY COULD BE THE
DAY THAT YOU ACCELERATE TOWARD THE
PERSON AND LIFE GOD HAS JUST FOR YOU.

Pain, you see, has a purpose. Sometimes it protects us or breaks us, directs us or re-directs us, stops us or causes us to move quickly. So, if this is true, how can we use pain for good?

I have found that pain lays us bare—wide open before others. If we allow it, pain can accelerate influence, not from an ambitious standpoint but from the standpoint of service. Leading is serving; it is the embodiment of ministry. We serve first; influence is what follows. So pain can influence someone toward intimacy with God or reconciliation with a spouse or peace between rivals. Pain is the broad embrace of a God who can turn any situation for His glory.

At the end of the day, the development *in* my life and the influence *from* my life depend on pain. Remember, a defining moment could be as close as the next painful experience.

So, if pain is indeed a constant companion, why not make friends with him? A.W. Tozer said, "It is doubtful that God can bless a man greatly until He has hurt him deeply."

I have a few helpful hints that I've learned while dealing with my own pain. They are short and sweet, but they've helped me time and again. Here they are:

1 LISTEN CAREFULLY

Is the pain you are working through right now healthy pain? If so, what is it that can be learned? Is there a nugget of truth inside your storm of confusion that can be used to help you? The voice of pain can help us learn or unlearn life lessons that prove valuable in the long run.

2 SUCK IT UP

Do not be afraid to hurt. Do not shy away from decisions that may lead you to pain. Give yourself permission to take some risks. Craig Groeschel also told me, "Often the difference between where we are and where God wants us to be is the pain we are unwilling to endure." We must be willing to increase our pain threshold or else we, as leaders, will limit our influence.

3 TALK IT OUT

Don't become a hermit. Too often we retreat to the inside, hiding our pain from those who can help us the best. Find a friend or a counselor. Do not walk life's journey by yourself. I know some people that feel that if they say they need help it is declaring weakness. If so, what is wrong with being weak? Remember, God is strongest when we are weakest. (see 2 Corinthians 12:9)

4 GIVE IT AWAY

What you hold on to is what you believe you can control. What you release is what you believe you need help with. I love the hope in 1 Peter 5:7, "Give all your worries and cares to God, for he cares about you." (NLT)

5 MOVE FORWARD

Do not allow pain to restrain you. There is so much in front of you that beckons your attention, your skills, and your time. Today could be the day that you accelerate toward the person and life God has just for you. ⬛

HIS WILL, NOT YOURS
AN INTERVIEW WITH FRANCIS CHAN

BY TIMOTHY WILLARD

WE SPEND SO MUCH TIME SETTING OURSELVES UP THAT WE REALLY DON'T HAVE TIME TO SAY, "OK, GOD, WHERE CAN I GO? WHERE DO YOU WANT ME TO GO?" INSTEAD WE SAY, "OK, GOD, I'LL GO ANYWHERE AS LONG AS YOU SET ME UP HERE WITH RETIREMENT, WITH THIS STANDARD OF LIVING FOR THE REST OF MY LIFE." THERE'S THIS WHOLE "I WILL GO ANY-WHERE *IF*." I THINK WE HAVE PLENTY OF *"IFS"* THAT KEEP US FROM PURSUING OUR CALLING.

Willard: Why is it that so many people miss out on their "true calling" in our culture?

Chan: I think there are a couple of reasons for this. Most people don't really care what their true calling is or what they were created for. We don't take verses like Colossians 1:16 literally: "... all things were created by him and for him." (NIV) We don't even think about the fact that we were made for Him, that we exist to serve Him.

We get so wrapped up in survival or our own wills and desires that we miss out on our calling. Often the most important thing to us is raising our family, getting them set up well, which leads me to the second reason why I think we miss out on our calling: we lack faith. We spend so much time trying to set ourselves up to live without faith because we live in a culture that affords us the ability to be self-sufficient.

Israel wasn't a culture where you could do that. Israel had to depend on God for the rains and the sun to come at the right times. Prayers of dependence were built into their year because they had to trust God for their sustenance. Literally.

Most people on the earth think like Israel, but in the U.S. we don't have to. In the U.S. we can set ourselves up so we don't have to live by faith. We don't want to have to worry about the future, and this idea of living by faith drives us crazy. It's selfish, really.

So, we defend all the reasons in the world why we don't have to live that way and shouldn't live that way. And we spend so much time setting ourselves up that we really don't have time to say, "OK, God, where can I go? Where do You want me to go?" Instead we say, "OK, God, I'll go anywhere as long as You set me up here with retirement, with this standard of living for the rest of my life." There's this whole "I will go anywhere *if*." I think we have plenty of *ifs* that keep us from pursuing our calling.

Willard: Talk about the difference between calling and giftedness. Is there a difference? Do most people rely on a skill set, rather than a calling?

Chan: If you look at Paul, who was an extremely gifted and knowledgeable man, when he went to the Corinthians, somehow he resolved to know nothing except Christ and Him crucified. He basically set some of his natural ability aside in order to accomplish *the will of God* in order to preach the foolishness of the cross.

It seems like he had wisdom to know when to hold back on his giftedness. If I were as intelligent as he was I probably would use that knowledge whenever it suited me. But somehow he had a wisdom and "a knowing" that I'm assuming was of the Spirit. He knew God wanted him to preach a certain way, which maybe was different from what he could have done based on his giftedness.

I also want to be careful with spending too much time trying to think, "Is this my calling? Is this my giftedness?" because the Bible doesn't really talk about this much at all. What we tend to do in Christian circles is maybe overthink certain things. It's easier to have "theological discussions" like that than it is to get our hands dirty.

Paul had this mindset that said, "I've got to glorify God whether I'm eating or drinking, and if He's given me some gifts, let me use those." Likewise, I'd like to see Christians saying, "What can I do for You right now? How can I use this afternoon or this ten minutes for You?" Let's not get too preoccupied debating "calling." I think if our hearts are seeking to glorify God—aligning with His desires—then we are going to find right results.

Willard: What can people do to align their desires with God's?

Chan: If we're constantly and regularly in the Scriptures then whatever situation we're in the Holy Spirit brings those Scriptures to mind. And when we encounter Scripture we are faced with a choice: either we take it *literally* or we explain away an action that we need to take.

If you're in an impoverished area or a third world country and you say, "OK, I'm going to love this person like Jesus." *Love like Jesus*, that's hard to do—there's some crazy action that needs to take place. But that's what happens when Scriptures come to mind. We must take action or remain static. So the main thing to consider is how much time are you in the Word for yourself meditating on those verses?

Willard: If you were sitting in front of a Catalyst leader who is struggling with "God's calling" on their life, what would you tell them?

Chan: I would tell them to be careful with this phrase "sense of calling." We need to focus first on *obedience* and seriously look at our lives. The Bible talks a lot more about obedience, which prompts questions like:

Is there something in my life right now that I'm not obedient to? What are those things?

In Luke 8, right after the parable of the soils, Jesus explains how we listen to the Word and how we respond to the Word, and then in verse 18 He says, "Be careful … how you listen. For to him who has will more be given; and from him who does not have, even what he thinks … he has will be taken away." (AMP)

So, we need to be careful how we hear God's Word because if there's not an obedience and a surrender to what we do know, why is He going to tell you anything new? First we've got to look at God's Word to see what we're disobedient to, because if God's going to speak to me and lead me and give me a strong conviction of my calling, it's going to be because I've been faithful or am seeking to be faithful to the things I know of in Scripture.

In 2 Chronicles 6:7-9, Solomon says:

My father David had it in his heart to build a temple for the Name of the LORD, the God of Israel. But the LORD said to my father David, 'Because it was in your heart to build a temple for my Name, you did well to have this in your heart. Nevertheless, you are not the one to build the temple, but your son.' (NIV)

David desired to do the right thing for the Lord, but God said, "That's great, you had good intentions, I'm so glad you had that in your heart, but that's not really *My will*. My will is that Solomon will build it."

I love this thought that God would say to me, "You know, Francis, you thought that you were going to build this church in the inner-city, and I'm glad it was in your heart. Nevertheless, that wasn't really what I wanted you to do, and that's not really the way it's going to happen."

I take that as a guide in my life. I'm trying to be obedient and do everything to the glory of God. This perspective allows me to serve the local church passionately with my gifts with whatever I think God might be calling me to with the right heart—for the glory of God.

When that happens then I think God will direct me and turn to me and say, "Great job, I'm glad it was in your heart, but that's not really what I want you to do. But keep going about it that way." **C**

HAITI:
A RETROSPECTIVE

All Haiti photography courtesy of Carmen Vaught.

WHITTLING COMPASSION:
HONING A "CONCERN"

BY JEDD MEDEFIND

June marked the half-year anniversary since Haiti's catastrophic earthquake. Aside from the small uptick in coverage at the milestone, the eyes of the world have largely turned elsewhere: oil leaks, soccer matches, November elections. Of course, this was all but inevitable. The 24-hour news cycle is fueled by "new," and tales of ongoing struggle, grinding poverty, and a less-than-hoped-for rebuilding are anything but new.

There's certainly good reason for frustration at the reality every news programmer knows all too well: news consumers rarely remain interested in other people's tragedy for more than a few months, at most. Such is human nature, as much a testimony to evil in our world as Haiti's earthquake itself. The truth is, if we tried to sustain concern for every tragedy we've ever seen on TV, we'd melt like cheese on a stovetop. So, as the media's conveyor belt of heartbreaking stories rolls on, we are left making uneasy peace with an emotional journey that looks like an EKG: long stretches of numbed apathy spiked by occasional moments of empathetic sorrow. Is this really the best way to live?

DIVIDED ATTENTION

When I was seven or eight, I loved to whittle. For starters, it was one of the few uses I could find for my first Swiss Army pocket knife. Then there was the satisfaction of *purposeful reduction*, refining a lumpy-ended stick into a spear tip or dagger. Curling flakes of raw wood piled up around my feet as a good-for-little knob became a point sharp enough, I imagined, to pierce a crocodile hide.

Is there any chance we'd want to take a Swiss Army knife to our blunt, lumpy-ended compassion? Might we want to shave off most of our good-for-little hand-wringing about the world's myriad problems, working to refine our thoughts and actions to a spear point?

At first, pulling back from general concern about tragedies might seem to diminish our compassion. Isn't there some virtue in feeling a pang of sadness at the plight of a fellow human? Perhaps. Yet when a similar pang is felt over and over again—often sandwiched between commercials for toothpaste and potato chips, and almost always producing no action in response— one rightly wonders, "What for?"

In such times, the God-given emotional response to human anguish—sorrow—evaporates into a mist of sentimentality. A stab of grief or tears brushed away with the back of a forefinger may give us a pleasant reassurance that we are, after all, compassionate people. Yet repeatedly feeling such emotions without responding does nothing for the world and may do even worse to us. As C.S. Lewis put it in *The Screwtape Letters*, "The more often [a person] feels without acting, the less he will be able ever to act …"

Troublingly, the glut of stories and images that we encounter daily makes this outcome almost inevitable. From radio to Internet to TV, we encounter dozens if not hundreds of tragedies each week. Ultimately, what this creates is *continual stimulation of compassion* without obvious *opportunity for response*. The result is a fractionalizing of attention, emotion, and action.

We see a parallel to the long-term consequences of this reality in the splintered mental processes of today's extreme multi-taskers. A Stanford study last year offered a surprising window into what results from ever-smaller divisions of focus. As one would anticipate, multi-taskers were found to have feeble capacity to concentrate or carry on sustained activity. Unexpectedly, however, multi-taskers also scored very poorly at multi-tasking itself. The habit of dividing attentions between multiple things seems to have made multi-

taskers worse at everything. "The huge finding is, the more media people use the worse they are at using any media," expressed one of the study's researchers. "We were totally shocked."

This irony, however, is not so rare after all. Who would argue that a young Casanova truly knows how to love a woman simply because he loves *many* women? With such a man, splintered affection is far less than the sum of its parts. To love well, as to do well, requires focus.

AN INVITATION

Quakers speak of a concept I've come to value deeply in recent years: what they refer to simply as a *concern*— the idea that from among all the many needs calling for our attention, there is often one that God invites us individually to engage. Although Scripture's explicitness on this point may be debated, it strikes me as a very natural extension of the biblical view of individual gifting (as in Romans 12 and 1 Corinthians 12) and the "good works, which God prepared beforehand, that we should walk in them." (Eph. 2:10 ESV)

A *concern* is an invitation to special focus, to ongoing concentration of thought and action. Certainly, other needs arise that require attention as well, from family illness to a stranger with a dead car battery. But most of the time, the concern serves as a focal point of ministry and service, enabling a person to pour herself wholeheartedly into the work God has given her. It is an enormous "yes" to one thing, and a freeing "not now" to the rest.

Seeking after a concern may offer just the Swiss Army knife we need to begin whittling. It's not that we cease to care about all the other ache and anguish in the world. I remember how my grandmother, every time she heard a siren, quietly prayed for the emergency workers rushing to the scene and those needing their aid. We'd do well to extend that practice to cover every tragic story encountered in the news as well. But with a concern, we can also be free to offer such prayer and then return focus to what God has uniquely given us, from mentoring foster youth across town to funding water wells in Africa.

TRUE CONCERN

A true concern is a gift—given, not seized. Most often, I believe, it is but a whisper of God's still, small voice: *This is the special burden, and special joy, I wish to give to you.*

A TRUE CONCERN IS A GIFT—
GIVEN, NOT SEIZED. MOST OFTEN,
I BELIEVE, IT IS BUT A WHISPER
OF GOD'S STILL, SMALL VOICE:
THIS IS THE SPECIAL BURDEN,
AND SPECIAL JOY, I WISH TO
GIVE TO YOU. THERE'S NEVER
BEEN A TIME WHEN I'VE HEARD
AUDIBLE WORDS FROM GOD.

There's never been a time when I've heard audible words from God. But I can say unequivocally that He has mysteriously woven my experiences, relationships, strengths, interests, and seemingly disconnected events to bring me to a true concern at many points in life.

Solitude and prayer play a key role in preparing us to receive this gift. Amidst a world flooded with stimulants and information, one of wisdom's most significant functions is simply to pick needles of significance from haystacks of noise. James urges, "If any of you lacks wisdom, let him ask God … and it will be given him." (James 1:5) That's what's required here. As a concern begins to arise, focused prayer for the issue itself also helps refine and confirm our sense of calling to engage it.

Intertwined with prayer, I've found times in solitude indispensable. Apparently, Jesus did too, spending the night before He chose His disciples alone on a mountainside, as He did so many other times. For me, at least, it is not so much that times in solitude—whether a half hour in the morning or a day alone in the mountains—immediately "produce" a clear calling. There have been such moments. But usually, it simply seems that regularly practicing time alone with God slows the dizzying merry-go-round of daily life, enabling me to see and hear Him more clearly in all things.

Finally, although the quest for a concern calls for both seeking and waiting (equally strong biblical themes held in tension with each other), I think it's worth noting that we need not remain paralyzed until we find what we imagine to be a lifetime calling. So many Gen X and Y-ers drift through years or more waiting for the "perfect fit" of a job or cause. The presence of endless options leads us to choose none, fearing we'll miss the "right path" if we start down another.

But concerns can change over time, often providing unexpected preparation for the future as well. A few years in city government may be the perfect training ground for discipleship ministry, and vice versa. The far greater mistake would be to waste those years engaging with little passion in tasks of little value. It is the equivalent of saying to the Master, "I was afraid and went out and hid your talent in the ground."

Instead, we must take His talents and invest, pouring them into a God-honoring undertaking guided by the unique concern He's given us. This begins and grows in prayer. But as God helps us whittle our cauliflower-shaped compassion into a focused point, we can engage His world in a way we never could before. We are released, perhaps for the first time, from the guilty hand-wringing over all the things we're not doing. Most importantly, our emotions and actions are honed to a spear tip sharp enough to pierce the hide of a crocodile. ◼

LET US
NOT FORGET

PHOTOGRAPHY BY CARMEN VAUGHT

A FOREVER THRONE

BY JONATHAN MERRITT

Many years ago, author William Martin wrote the authorized biography of Billy Graham titled, *A Prophet With Honor*. Throughout the almost eight hundred page book, he recounts numerous conversations with the famed preacher who perhaps touched more souls than any other in the last century. Toward the end of the book Martin sat down with Dr. Graham to ask him one question, which he had purposely saved for last:

What one word would you like people of future generations to use when they characterize your life and your ministry?

Martin said he purposely saved this question for last, and the striking gravity of the question explains why. He reports that the great preacher thought only for a moment before responding with a nugget of wisdom:

"Snapping his head slightly as if to lock into position to fire precisely at a key-target, he thrust out his jaw and said, 'Integrity! That is what I have worked for all my life: Integrity.'"[1]

If Graham could choose only one thing that would memorably mark his ministry, he says it would not be crowds or converts, but integrity. Yet one must wonder how many leaders today desire the same thing. If we could choose what might mark our lives, what would we

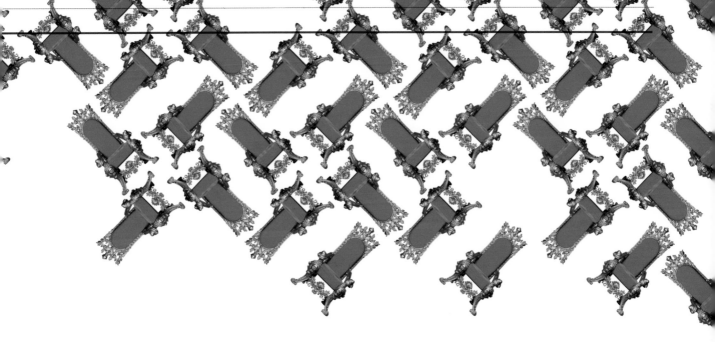

choose? Influence? Legacy? Or the little rewarded but always noticed character quality of integrity?

We are experiencing a crisis of integrity that is drenched in corporate and political scandals and set to the soundtrack of bootlegged music. Our world in the last decade has been especially riddled with lies from Madoff to Abramoff, from Enron to Goldman Sachs.

It's easy to cast stones at such failures, but we need to do the hard work of analyzing those trends that are fueling the breakdown of integrity in culture. What is causing us to compromise the characteristic that Graham feels is supremely important? Culturally speaking, there are at least three trends at work here.

THE ROOTS OF OUR DUPLICITY

Pragmatism. According to the New York Times, America leads the world in workplace productivity. But we didn't get there by accident. In the 20th century, American thinkers like John Dewey, Charles Peirce, and William James began developing an influential way of thinking known as pragmatism. This paradigm, now an earmark of American culture, seeks to make decisions based on something's usefulness and ability to deliver the desired result. From the church growth movement to metrics-obsessed managers, pragmatism continues to bear down on us.

The problem with this way of thinking is that it assumes that what works is right or best. For example, I know a church that offered expensive gift cards to members who brought first-time visitors. By essentially paying people to bring their friends to church that day, this congregation hit record high attendance, but one might argue that they lost much more. By valuing the goals over the means, we open ourselves up to decisions that might compromise our character.

Declining Creativity. A recent *Newsweek* cover story declared, "For the first time, research shows that American creativity is declining." According to the Torrence test of our nation's "creative quotient," our creativity has been falling for the last twenty years. The effects of the decline are visible. Marketplace brands are virtually indistinguishable from each other, and children regularly rely on prepackaged video game experiences rather than employing their imaginations.

To keep up with everyone else in this environment, we are tempted to steal the ideas of others rather than tap into our own. A great example is the American church. If you walk into many churches today, their striking similarities will make you feel like they are all nothing more than an emulation of some invisible standard. The sermon series is usually a rip-off of the latest summer

IN 1 KINGS 9:4-5, GOD TOLD THE FUTURE KING SOLOMON, "AS FOR YOU, IF YOU WALK BEFORE ME FAITHFULLY WITH INTEGRITY OF HEART AND UPRIGHTNESS, AS DAVID YOUR FATHER DID, AND DO ALL I COMMAND AND OBSERVE MY DECREES AND LAWS, I WILL ESTABLISH YOUR ROYAL THRONE OVER ISRAEL FOREVER..."

blockbuster movie, grungy fonts besiege you from all directions, and the pastor has clearly plagiarized half his sermon. Trapped in a creative vacuum and desperately wanting to produce results, we often produce the desired façade at the expense of our character.

Image Obsession. Any public relations firm can tell you that perception is everything today. If you don't maintain the right image, your brand can falter and the next thing you know, you're looking for a job. But for Christians, image isn't everything. We must be careful not to sacrifice our integrity on image's altar.

A great example of what not to do is the Catholic church's handling of the sex abuse scandal. Concerned with their image and the way the church might be perceived, some in the church responded to allegations of sexual misconduct by ignoring them, silencing them, or making them go away. Even as reports of incidents reached as high as eight hundred in one year, priests were quietly transferred and victims were paid off. In the end, the cover-up did more to tarnish their image and compromise their integrity than doing the right thing from the start.

NOTHING TO HIDE

In the face of such cultural trends, Scripture speaks powerfully. Again and again, its pages remind us that we need to maintain integrity despite the changes around us or the fallout will be great. In 1 Kings 9:4-5, God told the future King Solomon, "As for you, if you walk before me faithfully with integrity of heart and uprightness, as David your father did, and do all I command and observe my decrees and laws, I will establish your royal throne over Israel forever, as I promised David your father when I said, 'You shall never fail to have a successor on the throne of Israel.'" (TNIV)

Though King Solomon arguably forgot this command from time to time, he went on to write in the book of Proverbs that integrity was the key to making sound decisions. "The integrity of the upright guides them, but the unfaithful are destroyed by their duplicity." (Proverbs 11:3)

Unfortunately, the Western Church in the last century hasn't always been a shining beacon of integrity. Each one of us can conjure up images of the teary-eyed televangelists and damning headlines, which continue to foster religious skepticism among non-Christians.

So on the one hand, we have several cultural trends pushing us to compromise our character; on the other hand, we have religious skepticism bearing down upon us and waiting for us to mess up. In such a moment, is there any characteristic more important than integrity?

When institutional distrust and religious skepticism reign, we have the choice to either hold fast to integrity or be destroyed by duplicity. If others put a tail on us, hide in our closets, or investigate our tax returns, they must find us in good standing. Leaders today must be honest in our business dealings, generous with our money, and true to our words. Like Graham, may we live the type of lives so that future generations would survey our legacies and find them marked by unquestionable integrity. ◼

FIND ME BIGGER

BY JON ADAMS

I'VE TALKED WITH HUNDREDS OF PEOPLE WHO THIRST TO DESIRE GOD MORE. IS PASSION FOR GOD DISCOVERED AT THE NEXT CONFERENCE, THE NEXT BOOK, OR EVEN THE NEXT ARTICLE THAT YOU READ? HOW CAN WE BECOME MORE DESIROUS OF GOD?

I am passionate about the Church. I am a pastor of a church in "the burbs" of Atlanta. I love pastoring our congregation, praying with people, and even going to visit friends and members in the hospital. I've asked myself over the years, "Jon, why are you so passionate about the Church?"

The answer that comes rifling back to me isn't always a pleasant one. Too often, my passion for the Church is connected with the passion for *my own name* to be promoted. But what if my passion for God actually equaled my passion for the Church ... or for my name? Then what would my ministry look like? How would this *God passion* affect my family and all of life?

HIS RISING NAME
Throughout the Bible, we are taught that honoring the name of the Lord is synonymous with giving credit or a special place in our hearts for God and His entire character. For example, in Acts 4:12 it says, "And there is salvation in no one else, for there is no other name under heaven given among men by which we must be saved." (ESV)

The name by which we are saved is none other than the entire person and work of Jesus.

In the small book of Malachi the prophet writes, "From the rising of the sun to its setting my name will be great among the nations." (Malachi 1:11) Throughout Malachi and the entire Bible, heavy emphasis is placed on honoring the name of God. God is a jealous God, passionate about His own glory and fame. He is *the* Creator God, and deserves our praise and honor. But He also wants you and I to be passionate about His fame and glory as well, living lives filled with ardor and reverence for Him.

And that's what we want too. I have talked with hundreds of people who thirst to desire God more. Is passion for God discovered at the next conference, in the next book, or even the next article that you read? How can we become more *desirous* of God? Scripture reminds us that the more we focus on honoring the Name of the Lord, the more our hearts will be filled with passion for Him.

A GROWING HEART
When my girls were little, I used to read them C.S. Lewis' *The Chronicles of Narnia*. In the second book, *Prince Caspian*, the little British girl Lucy enters Narnia again and sees Aslan for the first time after not seeing him for a very long time. They have a beautiful reunion and Lucy questions the great Lion, "Aslan, you're bigger now." Aslan replies, "Lucy, that's because you are older. You see, Lucy, every year that you grow, you will find me bigger."[1]

THE PRACTICE FORCES ME TO BUILD IN A DAILY PRAYER RE-PRIEVE TO REMIND ME OF HOW GREAT HIS NAME REALLY IS.
I CAN ALMOST FEEL MY HEART FILLING WITH DESIRE FOR HIM.

That's what I want. I want Jesus to become bigger in my heart and my passion for Him to grow exponentially as I continue through life's journey. But how do we increase our passion for God? We need to grow in how we make His name great in our lives. This is a lifelong process, but we can learn how to daily push praise in His direction in a more constant, consistent way. Here are two thoughts on the matter.

SAY "NO" TO SOUND BITE THEOLOGY AND PRACTICES

We want fast, quick-fix answers to grow in our passion for God. Passion can be found "in the moment," but such passion is ephemeral. Lasting desire for God is developed the same way that we grow any relationship: investing and cultivating a relationship over time.

I'm not talking about finding the right method, but simply admitting that this thing called passion and intimacy with God is a journey in a relationship. It's taken me years (and I'm still learning tons) about how my wife feels loved and affirmed by me. When she is happy, the whole family is happy, including me. We need to begin pursuing God in our churches the way we pursue our spouses (or significant others).

A few years ago, God was waking me up three to five nights a week in the middle of the night. When this first happened, I didn't recognize it was God waking me. But after it happened several times, I decided to read and meditate on a Psalm and then pray the Psalm back to the Lord in my own words. This became a conversation with God and my heart grew with passion and joy in the midst of our evening rendezvous. I actually began praying that God would wake me up.

REST

Saturday used to be known as "The Preparation Day" for the Christian Sabbath or what became known as "The Lord's Day." You may or may not buy into a Sabbath principle: one day of rest out of seven. But, whether you practice Sabbath rest or not, we all need to grow in our understanding of what biblical rest is and how it replenishes our passion for God and His kingdom.

Recently, what has actually become more restful to me has been practicing fixed hour prayer. This is the ancient practice of pausing throughout the day to reflect on the Word of God and to remember Him through practicing prayers and hymns of the ancients. I have found that to remain consistent in practicing fixed hour prayer (morning, middle day, vespers, and late night prayers called "compline") I have to hit the pause button in my busy schedule. The practice forces me to build in a daily prayer reprieve to remind me of how great His name really is. I can almost feel my heart filling with desire for Him.

As I consider my personal alone thoughts—what drives me—I still find that *my name* is still way too central in my thinking. But, I'm growing, and I love the passion that God is filling my heart with as I seek to make His Name and glory more central in my life. C

THE
ANTHROPOLOGIST

BY TIMOTHY WILLARD

Down the old access road you run into the horizon. It burns your eyes with orange and red, some purple. The autumn air forces the memories out of your brain; you stand, a solitary silhouette in the dimming light. Your eyes blur the colors and memories with tears.

Back at the house, the fire dwindles. Feet scamper and laughter bounces down the stairs. You stoke the fire and sit on the floor—the laughter, the sunset, the crackle. Life feels huge all bottled up in your little room of eternity. "They're already asleep," she says. "Try and get some rest."

But your sunset experience and subsequent return to reality collide. You needed to breathe, just for a moment. Now, though, reality digs in: layoffs looming at work, you have tough decisions to make, plus your dad's back in the hospital. You once heard a pastor talk about how life's tension drives people toward God. But the only place you feel driven toward is the edge.

MORE THAN IMAGE

In film, conflict drives every scene. Each character moves toward their goal and must, often times, go through hell to reach that goal. Viewers resonate with films that perform this task well—we love being drawn into the tension and conflict of the characters' story.

GOD ALLOWS REALITY'S TENSION TO BEAR DOWN ON US AS A MEANS TO DRIVE US TOWARD HIM.

Why do we love it when the hero overcomes their adversity, their conflict?

We love it because we can relate. We love it because something exists in every person that urges them toward what is beyond the seemingly impossible.

The Teacher of Ecclesiastes alludes to this transcendent notion in chapter 3 verse 11: "He has planted eternity in the human heart, but even so, people cannot see the whole scope of God's work from beginning to end." (NLT) Though we can *perceive* the obscurity of the eternal, we get frustrated because we still cannot fathom its meaning. And this is no good when the realities of life stare us down and drive us toward the edge.

King David's words sound good when reality rages: "[God] Why do you bother with us?" (Psalm 8:4, *The Message*) But God *does* bother with us. In that same Psalm David recognizes the gifts that God gave to man: making him a little lower than gods, in control

of creation. God did not merely make man to bear His image. He made man to relate to Him, to talk with Him, to walk with Him, to love Him.

God allows reality's tension to bear down on us as a means to drive us toward Him. It's like the Teacher says, "God does it so that we will fear Him." So, we are more than image bearers. We are participants wrapped in holy relationship with God.

THE RIVERS NEVER FILL

A sense of waste, however, emerges as we stumble through life's tension. These kinds of feelings make leading difficult. Leaders are supposed to inspire others toward a common goal--something greater than themselves. But it is possible to feel overcome with purposelessness. Our vocations and goals can all get wound into a confusing ball of "Why do I even try?" Early on in his cultural experiment, the Teacher of Ecclesiastes discovered that God "dealt a tragic existence to the human race." (Eccl. 1:13 NLT) From his

I'VE ALSO CONCLUDED THAT WHATEVER GOD DOES, THAT'S THE WAY IT'S GOING TO BE, ALWAYS. NO ADDITION, NO SUBTRACTION. GOD'S DONE IT AND THAT'S IT. THAT'S SO WE'LL QUIT ASKING QUESTIONS AND SIMPLY WORSHIP IN HOLY FEAR.

vantage point, everything humanity strives for is like running after the wind.

The rivers run into the ocean but the ocean never fills. The sun rises and sets and does it again and again. And meanwhile, the generations toil and die off. And for what? Nothing.

We feel like that too—caught in a never-ending cycle. Even as Christians we can fall victim to meaninglessness. But the Teacher, though he makes these observations objectively, does not make them through the lens of the eternal God. Only after his tirade in the first two and a half chapters does he finally offer insight that makes his anthropological study shimmer with hope:

I've decided that there's nothing better to do than go ahead and have a good time and get the most we can out of life. That's it—eat, drink, and make the most of your job. It's God's gift. I've also concluded that whatever God does, that's the way it's going to be, always. No addition, no subtraction. God's done it and that's it. That's so we'll quit asking questions and simply worship in holy fear. Whatever was, is. Whatever will be, is. That's how it always is with God. (Eccl. 3:14-15, *The Message*)

Often, our sense of entitlement and need for recognition and glory interrupt our view of life. Instead of seeing through His eternal lens, we get stuck pursuing and pursuing, ignorant that life is not about us. It's about how we relate to Him.

THE GRACE LENS

The Teacher ends his book by encouraging his readers to keep an eternal focus: fear God, listen to His Word. For us, His Word does not manifest itself in the Old Testament Law like it would have for the Teacher's readers. We have the blessedness of living each day in relationship with God because of the redemptive work of Christ. Now we not only see reality through an eternal lens but through the lens of grace. And grace comes when we need it most; it comes free and is never ending.

So as we lead in our vocations and other endeavors, our relationship with Christ paints our perspective. We can see further into the sunset and know there is peace on the other side of the coming tension. We may not be able to understand any of it—why God allows certain things into our lives—but we can trust in His sovereignty.

Community in leadership is not only about establishing a good rapport with those you serve and lead. It is aligning yourself with God's eternal perspective. It's about cultivating a relationship that governs all other relationships found under the umbrella of your community. It is easy to lose faith in the Eternal when the present reality won't let you sleep. But always remember the end of the matter: fall on your face before God and abide in Christ.

.....

You find yourself down the old access road yet again. Winter bites hard now, but not as hard as your recent reality. You had to say good-bye to some great people at work, and your dad is not improving. The sun already sleeps and the gray moves into the trees. For some reason, you can still see fine. You hear laughter down the lane. You feel the cold—how it pushes you inward.

"Are you OK?" she squeezes your hand.

"Yeah … yeah." ◼

CHURCH.
WHY GO?

BY MARGARET FEINBERG

People grow in their relationship with God in a myriad of ways. For me, reading the Bible, prayer, and connecting to God through spiritual disciplines reignites my faith and renews my hope in the One who was, is, and forever will be. While church* has definitely played a role in my spiritual formation—especially during the early years—I found my desire to attend a local church has waned over time.

This has been exacerbated by the transient nature of my life, which includes five major moves over the last ten years. With each new city, finding a church became increasingly difficult. Like dating, searching for a church home can be awkward, uncomfortable, and even unbearable—especially if you lose your sense of humor.

After settling into a home church, I struggled with the gap of what the church is and what it could be. I've wondered why some churches are more concerned with style than substance and marketing than making disciples. I firmly believe that small groups are good, but more often than not I've found myself in gatherings that lack depth, real connection, or a willingness to put faith into action.

As a result, my own desire to attend church decreased until I began to wonder, "Why do I even go at all?" I

tried to console myself with the fact that even Jesus went to church, although He didn't always like what He saw when He got there. But He still went.

THE GATHERING OF BELIEVERS

Nearly ten years ago, while taking care of my aunt's bed and breakfast in Alaska, I met an unforgettable woman named Lynne. She was a shepherdess.

Intrigued, I began peppering her with all kinds of questions about her flock and began drawing rich spiritual parallels between her descriptions and biblical teachings regarding sheep. I promised myself that one day I'd study this scriptural theme more in-depth.

Last year I decided to reconnect with Lynne. I reintroduced myself, and she invited me to spend a few days with her flock.

One day, standing in a muddy Oregon field with her flock, Lynne unknowingly reminded me of some of the most basic principles of why the gathering together of believers is essential. She explained that sheep are defenseless. They don't have sharp teeth or pointed hooves. Without protective features, their only defense is to flock together. That's why whenever a predator is nearby, a flock will gather closely.

"But what happens to the sheep that wanders off on its own?" I asked.

Lynne explained that those are the ones that get picked off by predators, infected by parasites, or overindulge in grass until they become ill. It's only within a flock under the watchful eye of a good shepherd that the sheep are protected and enjoy a healthy life.

I couldn't help but see the parallels between a flock and the church. From its foundation, Christianity has never been about isolation. In Genesis, we are given the profound observation that it is "not good" for man to be alone. This is the first mention within Scripture that something was "not good" and it's spoken in the context of the relationship between a man and woman. Yet I can't help but wonder if the statement reflects a basic life principle—we need one another.

Throughout the Old Testament, spiritual leaders are consistently given encouragement in the form of friends and followers. Moses and Aaron, David and Jonathan, Elijah and Elisha, Naomi and Ruth—just to name a few. Jesus' first act in ministry is to call twelve followers who will form a band of spiritual brothers. When the church is birthed in Acts (Acts 2:3-42), the Spirit descends on people who are gathering together.

BEING IN A CHURCH ISN'T EASY FOR MANY PEOPLE— INCLUDING ME. THE CHURCH, BY NATURE, IS INHERENTLY FLAWED. BUT IT'S IN THIS PLACE THAT I ENCOUNTER GOD IN UNEXPECTED WAYS.

What do these gathered people do after the tongues of fire fade? They keep gathering together. They teach the story of God. They sing. They share meals. They pray. They spend time together. Because of their common love of God, who is described as the Good Shepherd, they can't help but form a close-knit community.

Reflecting on these passages, I'm always intrigued by how little the Scriptures tell us about what they actually do when they're together. Sure, there's music, encouraging, teaching, and eating, but what about the format? The length? The location? The order? The time of day? The specific elements of the gathering seem far less important than *actually* gathering.

Unlike the sheep in Lynne's upper field, something far beyond safety happens when followers of Jesus come together. Throughout the New Testament, we are reminded of

the things God works in and through us as we live in community. Colossians 3:1-17 challenges us individually and corporately to live out our days in such a way that is pleasing to God. As the people of God, holy and wholly loved, we are to clothe ourselves with gentleness and patience, forgiving others (and ourselves) at every turn, overflowing with love and thankfulness. The apostle Paul writes:

"Let the word of Christ dwell in you richly as you teach and admonish one another with all wisdom, and as you sing psalms, hymns and spiritual songs with gratitude in your hearts to God." (Col. 3:15-17 NIV)

In the company of fellow believers, our own sinful nature, petty grievances, and selfish desires are exposed, not so that we become divided and bitter, but that we may be set free, redeemed, and created into all God has called and created us to be. The church becomes the formative foundation where we learn to live out the ministry of reconciliation. (2 Cor. 5:18)

As members of the body, we have the opportunity to grow together and learn how to function properly with our unique gifts, talents, and callings. Along the way, we garner strength for our own faith journey and we may even find that the gathering of Christians, the church, and this adventure of following Jesus is not only fun—but contagious! Our love and unity invite the world to know Christ. (John 17:21)

AMONG THE FLOCK

As we walked among the fields, Lynne explained that rivalries exist among the sheep. Ewes who have just given birth tend to be a possessive bunch. Rams are often at odds with each other—sometimes even dueling each other to death if they are outside the presence of the shepherd.

Watching the flock interact reminded me that sometimes it's tough to stick together in a confined area. Within a flock, sheep slow each other down, step on each other's hooves, and trip each other from time to time. Being in a flock has never been easy for sheep, but it's how they were designed to live and flourish.

In the same way, being in a church isn't easy for many people—including me. The church, by nature, is inherently flawed. But it's in this place that I encounter God in unexpected ways. Not only do I experience acceptance, forgiveness, grace, love, and compassion from fellow believers, but I am given the opportunity to extend them to others—even after they step on my toes. Within the church, I'm learning to appreciate many of the intangibles that emerge in the process of living everyday life together—learning to work through ups and downs, disagreements and tensions, innovations and failures. As we pursue God through life's potpourri of tragedies and triumphs, we learn to love more deeply and find ourselves becoming a little bit more like Jesus.

In this place called church, I rediscover that I am not alone on this Christian journey. I'm reminded that I only have a snapshot of the larger story of what God is doing in this generation and the grander story of what He has been doing throughout history. By adding my voice to the familiar chorus of "Amazing Grace," reciting from the *Book of Common Prayer*, celebrating the sacraments, or listening to the wisdom of John Wesley and those who have gone before, I partake in the beautiful story God has been unfolding since the beginning of time. And I am reminded that God has not failed us yet. Nor will He.

While I taste portions of these truths in my personal time with Christ and the Scripture, the flavor is never as wondrous as when I experience them in the presence of fellow believers. For these reasons and many more, I recognize that whether I like it or not I need the church. I can't be all I've been created to be on my own.

I'll see you on Sunday. **C**

*Church is loaded with meaning for many people. For the purposes of this article, I want to clarify that God has never been a building. I would like to sidestep the discussion of building, denomination, size, or liturgy, and focus on the church as the organic gathering of believers in whatever form that may take.

BELIEF
FAILURE

BY JOHN ORTBERG

"To believe is to begin to pray."

This one sentence, from a wonderful book on belief and unbelief by Michael Novak, will mess with the way you think about prayer. It also tells us how central prayer is in spiritual formation. It deals with what we *actually* believe, rather than what we merely *profess* to believe. And what we *actually* believe is what governs our life.

Novak does not say that if you become a believer you *ought* to begin to pray. He does not say that if you're a church leader you should learn about prayer or promote prayer or model prayer. Eugene Peterson once wrote that a big challenge of ministry is that it reinforces inattentiveness to God. People in our churches may complain if messages are bad or music stinks or the videos are lame, but they are not likely to complain if we are overly busy and spiritually under-nourished.

"To believe is to begin to pray." This means that if you believe—*really* believe, not just join a church or affirm a doctrine—it changes your understanding of the context in which you speak. Because if you begin to actually believe that there is a God who is always present and always listening, you begin to believe that you are never speaking off the grid.

MAYBE YOU PRAY MORE THAN YOU KNOW

Sometimes it helps to think in terms of any other form of personal communication. When it comes to speaking with another person, we can view three options:

1. I speak directly to Person A.

2. I speak *in the presence of* Person A.

In this case, I may be speaking to a third party. But I am keenly aware that Person A is standing in our little group, and is listening to each word I say. Even though my words don't address Person A, they are shaped by my awareness of his presence.

3. I speak *in the absence of* Person A.

In this case Person A cannot see or hear me. Have you ever said anything about a person in their absence that you would not have said if they were present?

Now back to God.

I can speak directly to God.

I can speak to another person *in the presence* of God.

IT IS SOBERING TO THINK THAT SOMETIMES I MAY THINK I HAVE BEEN PRAYING WHEN REALLY I'M JUST ENGAGED IN THE SUPERSTITIOUS ADDRESSING OF THE DEITY OF THE THUMBS GAME.

But I *cannot* speak *in the absence* of God.

We forget this. And sometimes those of us who are "professional Christians" forget it most of all.

THUMBS UP

I attended a Christian college where we always prayed in the cafeteria before eating. In order to determine who would pray, students commonly played "the thumbs game." When they sat down, everyone would turn their thumbs up in the air. Whoever *lost* the thumbs game was the person who would pray.

The pray-er would say something like this: "Dear God, thank You that we get to pray to You. What a privilege it is to pray …"

I imagine God saying: "If it's such a privilege, why does the *loser* of the thumb game get stuck doing it?"

It is as if we thought of God as being incommunicado while we were playing the thumbs game, and then suddenly coming into radio contact when we bowed our head and shut our eyes to pray. As if He were at the other end of a video monitor that was controlled by us.

The thumbs game is not just a poor way to pick a pray-er. It is evidence of a failure in *belief*. If I'm living with a God whose consciousness can be turned on and off by bowed heads and closed eyes, no wonder I will find it difficult to take such prayer seriously.

Jesus had a fundamentally different belief, and therefore a different experience of prayer. He actually believed that His father was always present.

This is why, when Jesus was healing somebody, He would sometimes address the person He was healing, and sometimes address His Father. In fact, when He was calling Lazarus out of the tomb, He actually speaks to this exact issue: "Father, I thank you that you have heard me. I knew that you always hear me, but I said this for the benefit of the people standing here, that they may believe that you sent me." (John 11:41b-42 NIV)

Jesus never said a word out of the hearing of His Father. So it did not matter a great deal whether He was addressing His Father or another person. For Jesus, the line between praying and just talking became exceedingly thin.

In fact, that line was pretty much erased.

JOYFUL AWARENESS

To believe is to begin to pray.

This means that my understanding of the goal of prayer changes. If someone were to ask you what the goal of your prayer life consists of, what would you say?

If I want to be serving in the ministry of Jesus, then I want to enter into the prayer life of Jesus.

That means my goal is not to pray longer, or more often. My goal is not to wear out my knees. My goal is not to be something called "a prayer warrior."

My goal is to learn to speak every word in the joyful awareness of the presence of the Father.

Jesus once said to religious leaders, "By your words you will be condemned." (Matthew 12:37 NKJV) I used to think that meant don't speak any unnecessary words. But what He really means is that it's the words you speak when you are not trying to be spiritual—when you think you are not praying—that reveal the true condition of your heart. This is why some people can think of themselves as great prayers but the reality is they are a long way away from home.

I don't know all that this means for you.

Maybe it means finding more time to be alone to pray. Maybe it means finding the right place. A friend of mine prays best when having long walks on the beach. Maybe it means doing more praying with other people.

I do know one thing for sure: it means making "praying" and "just talking" a lot more connected with each other.

NON-LINEAR CHAOS

I was at a meeting recently with a group of people that included a man who had just retired from 47 years in local church ministry. He had us pray for each other, with each other—with our eyes open, and our heads unbowed, while we went back and forth between addressing God and one another in a most chaotic and non-linear way. He said he finds himself doing this sort of thing more often these days.

As he reflects on almost five decades in church ministry, he cannot recall very many meetings of committees or teams or planning groups. He does not have many powerful memories of votes that decided carpet colors or song selections. But it is the sharing of hearts, and then the pouring out of hearts in prayer, that is most seared in his mind.

It is the heart speaking in the deep presence of brothers and sisters, and in the tender mercies of God, that still echoes when so much else of what we often think of as ministry has been silenced.

It is sobering to think that sometimes I may think I have been praying when really I'm just engaged in the superstitious addressing of the Deity of the Thumbs Game. But there's another side to prayer. It is just possible that your heart actually cries out to God more often than you think it does.

It may be that you pray more than you know.

To believe is to begin to pray. ◼

REARTICULATING
THE DIVINE

BY BRETT MCCRACKEN

I am a C. I am a C-H. I am a C-H-R-I-S-T-I-A-N. And I have C-H-R-I-S-T in my H-E-A-R-T and I will L-I-V-E E-T-E-R-N-A-L-L-Y . . ."

When I was a kid in Sunday school, that was my favorite song. Mostly because it was fun to sing but it was also a sort of creedal, confident, straight-to-the-point declaration of identity. Who am I? I am a C-H-R-I-S-T-I-A-N. Simple as that. It was a cool song to sing because "Christian" was a cool thing to be. It meant Jesus Christ was in my heart. It meant I was going to live eternally in his kingdom. What an amazing thing! Who would be ashamed to be a Christian?

But then I grew older and started to notice that a lot of Christians were really annoying, hypocritical, and, well, disappointingly human. A lot of them were hardly distinguishable from non-Christians. I knew of Christians who cheated on their wives, Christians who cursed and drank like sailors, teenage Christians who drove BMWs. I wondered what it really meant to be a Christian, beyond just "being saved," and why it might be something to be proud of and excited about.

When it comes down to it, this whole discussion about cool and Christianity concerns Christian identity. It explores who we are as Christians, how we conceive of our

role as the church and our identity in Christ, and how the world perceives us. Whether talking about wannabe or authentic Christian hipster communities, we ask these important questions: Do we know who we really are? From what source do we define ourselves? Is it the culture, the fashion magazines, the billboards or runways? Or is it God, Scripture, and theological tradition?

I think that the church has increasingly let itself be defined by the outside and by its own reactions to the culture at large. A by-product of so many developments in recent centuries (capitalism, consumerism, technology, postmodernism, democracy, advertising, etc.), this unfortunate situation has led the church to a place of looking to the outside for its internal direction. Whereas previous generations of Christians confidently asserted their identity in terms of *sola scriptura, sola fide, sola gratia, sola Christus,* and *soli Deo gloria* (by Scripture, faith, grace, Christ, and to God's glory alone), today's Christians are more apt, in their wayfaring, postmodern panic, to live by the *sola cultura* philosophy: by culture alone.

But why do we think it is a good idea to take our cues from culture? Is there anything more screwed up, incongruous, fractured, and inconsistent than the culture in which we live today? If, when we are talking about what is cool, we are referring to the fickle, fast-moving, over-before-it-started status symbols to which everyone (hipster or not) is captive, why would we ever spend so much time and energy fashioning our identity around it?

It's high time we take back our Christian identity from the clutches of marketing, consumerism, and the accompanying soulless bric-a-brac of mass-market capitalism. It's time we rediscover who we really are (and always have been) as the body of Christ.

There are three problems I see as contributing to our eroding sense of identity, and one solution.

PROBLEM #1:
REACTING TO RIPPLES

My little nephew Gabriel loves throwing rocks into rivers, ponds, and pretty much any body of water. The rock makes a fun plop noise, creates a splash, and in previously still waters creates ripples that push out from the center and get larger and larger the farther out they go. Everyone loves to make an impact and see its ramifications—to see that one little rock can ripple out to impact an area hundreds of times larger than its original size.

The ripple image can be aptly applied to Christianity in terms of how it started and what it has become. But these days, most "big ripple" events don't have much to do with Christianity. When was the last time you saw a world-shaking, viral phenomenon that stemmed from the church or began with a Christian? Our inside-out impact is increasingly negligible. More often than not, we are *reacting* to the impacts and ripples of the secular world ("GodTube" comes to mind). We are living according to the trends, ideas, technologies, and innovations trickling out from some distant, crucial center. And frequently we are among the last to receive the ripple message; we are on the outer rings.

Whenever Christians play copycat like this, whenever we define ourselves in this mimetic way, we do ourselves harm. We become just another subculture trying to appropriate pop culture for our own purposes. This imitative role reduces Christianity to a featherweight faith with so little internal combustion energy that it might very well topple over if the ripples and waves coming at it get too fast and furious. Dick Staub calls it "Christianity-Lite"—a faith that "has abandoned the mandate to build a richer intellectual and aesthetic culture on earth, choosing to settle for a mindless, insipid, imitative artistic subculture instead."[1]

PROBLEM #2:
SCRATCHING WHERE THEY ITCH

One of the most troubling things I see when I look at contemporary Christianity is the mentality that the church should fashion itself according to the needs and wants of the "audience." This idea grew out of the evangelical church growth and seeker movements and is practically an epidemic today. Almost every evangelical church thinks, to some extent, in terms of what the audience wants and how churches can provide them with a desirable product. This unseemly pressure to bow to the masses is just a symptom of the consumerist culture we live in. Presumably, it is simply how things must be done. Whatever else you might say about a product you're trying to sell, the one thing you know for sure is this: the audience is sovereign.

But of course, the question the church must reckon with is this: Is Christianity a product we must sell?

In the problematic "audience is sovereign" approach, audiences rarely want what is really in their best interest. A company might make money by giving the audience what they want, but this rarely satisfies the audience in the long run. And it hardly ever edifies their soul.

Furthermore, in terms of Christianity, what the audience wants has very little bearing on what Christianity actually is. In a market economy, consumer needs are those that *consumers* identify for themselves. But as David Wells points out, "The needs sinners have are needs *God* identifies for us, and the way we see our needs is rather different from the way he sees them. . . . The product we will seek naturally will not be the gospel."

Christianity is much bigger and above all earthly whims, fads, desires, and emotional cravings. If we think we can sell it best on the terms of the consumer, we are gravely mistaken.

PROBLEM #3:
MARKETING A NONCOMMERCIAL MESSAGE

The church today has a weakness for numbers. We are infatuated with measurements and quantified data: statistics, opinion polls, market research, attendance figures, bestseller lists, budgets, and so on. We want to monitor what the masses are buying, where the people are flocking, and what is hot right now, so that perhaps our warehouse churches will overflow with seeker-consumers. In other words, the church today operates like a corporation, with a product to sell and a market to conquer.

But what happens to our faith when we turn it into a product to sell? What does it mean to package Christianity in a methodical manner so as to make it salient to as wide an audience as possible? What does Christianity lose when it becomes just one piece of a consumer transaction? These are questions that the brand managers of cool Christianity would do well to consider.

Let's think for a minute about what Christianity is and why it doesn't make a good "product." For one thing, products must be subject to markets, yet God is not subject to the consumer needs or wants of any market. God only and ever deals on his own terms. His grace comes from within him, and he bestows it on us as he pleases. It doesn't come when we are ready for it or when we long for it. We struggle to fathom something that can't be purchased "on demand" in this day and age, but Christianity is one such thing. God saves at his discretion and on his watch.

Another reason why Christianity doesn't make a good product is that it doesn't lend itself to an easy commercial sale. Sure, there are appealing things about it, but there

LET'S THINK FOR A MINUTE ABOUT WHAT CHRISTIANITY IS AND WHY IT DOESN'T MAKE A GOOD "PRODUCT." FOR ONE THING, PRODUCTS MUST BE SUBJECT TO MARKETS, YET GOD IS NOT SUBJECT TO THE CONSUMER NEEDS OR WANTS OF ANY MARKET.

ALMOST EVERY EVANGELICAL CHURCH THINKS, TO SOME EXTENT, IN TERMS OF WHAT THE AUDIENCE WANTS AND HOW CHURCHES CAN PROVIDE THEM WITH A DESIRABLE PRODUCT.

are also not-so-appealing things about it (um . . . taking up one's cross, avoiding sin and worldliness, etc.). And although the gospel is wonderfully simple in the sense that even a child can recognize its truth, it is also mind-blowingly complex in a way that doesn't lend itself to thirty-second jingles.

Pop Christianity is on the verge of becoming little more than just another vacuous moniker and feel-better-about-myself, over-the-counter drug. It's always easier to consume cool or buy a satisfactory status (whether emotional, spiritual, or physical) than it is to legitimately work for it, earn it, and become it.

SOLUTION: FINDING OUR CORE

These three problems I've outlined stem from and underscore contemporary Christianity's identity crisis and fear-induced overcompensations for its increasingly marginalized place in culture.

The church's only way out of this quagmire, I believe, is to commit to rediscover and rearticulate its core, biblical purpose in the world, and to devote itself to being the divine and eternal body of Christ, not the flimsy and ephemeral thing the world wants it to be.

I'm convinced that most secular seekers today care very little about how cool church is, but very much about how authentic it is. They are interested in the church being the church. They want the church to know what it is and be honest with itself and the world, and to quit putting on airs of glossy marketability and perfection. People see through that. They know that Christianity—like anything else in life—is not perfect. They sense that Christianity is maybe inherently uncool and difficult to live out. But they also sense that it might actually be true, and they're waiting for the church to just speak that truth clearly to them, without all the distracting bells and whistles. **C**

THE NEW SHAPE
OF WORLD CHRISTIANITY
AN INTERVIEW WITH MARK NOLL

BY TIMOTHY WILLARD

Mark Noll became interested in the history of Christianity first as a way of understanding the Christian faith itself. Christian faith became important to him in college. He found many significant issues to examine from his own life. It seemed natural to look at the past for guidance.

After reading about the major figures of the Protestant Reformation, as well as the European history of Christianity and American history of Christianity, he was surprised to discover that if you enrolled in the right graduate program you could get paid to read and talk about it for a living.

Dr. Noll continues to engage in readings and discussions with interesting people. He mentioned that it flabbergasts him that he is still able to make his livelihood doing what he loves. Many of us are thankful for his timely contributions and hope he continues to reveal the extraordinary history of Christianity to us.

Willard: In your book *The New Shape of World Christianity*, you offer three views regarding how American Christianity has shaped world Christianity. Could you give us a synthesis of these views?

Noll: The way of looking at Christianity in the United States and then Christianity around the world can come in several different ways.

The point I tried to develop in the book, *The New Shape of World Christianity,* is to look at the history of the United States and what has happened to its Christian community and then compare that to the history of much of world Christianity today. I do not feel, as some would suggest, that the best way to think about believers in the U.S. is to regard them as dictating what happens around the rest of the world. There is, however, some connection and back and forth.

Willard: What makes the U.S. version of Christianity unique?

Noll: I think the way in which the Christian faith developed in the United States can explain much that's happening in the world today. United States Christian development is unusual because it existed without the state church establishments that had been in place everywhere in Europe.

The United States was not going to follow the European way. There were too many different forms of Protestantism and eventually Catholicism, Judaism, and so forth. There were also strong opinions, originally from the Baptists, the Quakers, and some of the Mennonites, that it was better for the churches not to have this kind of attachment.

As the freer form of Christian organization developed, the reliance upon voluntary means of supporting the churches worked very well. In fact, the great missionary expansion region of the world in the nineteenth century was the United States of America.

So I follow the real leaders in interpreting world Christianity, like Andrew Walls, in saying that what we have in nineteenth century American history is the emergence on the world scene of forms of Christianity that are almost entirely voluntaristic and almost entirely dependent on the free activity of the groups that contribute to the churches. Significant to that history for the present is that most of the major Protestant growth spurts in world Christianity today are developing in this pattern.

For example, Christianity has really taken off in China in the last forty years and it's in an American situation. That is to say, there's no help from the government, and there's no desire by the churches to run the government. In much of Africa over the course of the twentieth century, and especially since the end of colonization in 1916, that same situation has prevailed.

Occasionally an African government will support the churches, but mostly it's a free-form voluntary situation where the churches exist by the efforts and exertions of their own people. And that form borrows very much from the pattern of the United States.

The more complicated issue is to evaluate what's gained and what's lost, what's positive and what's negative, in this historical situation around the world.

Willard: Can you comment on some of those positives and negatives?

Noll: American Christian history for the last two centuries has been exemplary, especially by comparison with Europe, in the ability to draw lay people into active church life. It's been exemplary in the number of avenues opened up for women to take part, for example, in church life, church organization, and missionary life. It's been exemplary in levels of voluntary giving to the churches. In general you might say that the Protestant doctrine of the priesthood of all believers has finally come into its own in the U.S.

On the negative side, the energy, the innovation, and the creativity of the American churches has been historically averse to or not particularly interested in learning lessons from the past. This means that in the American church life there's been a lot of energy expended to create or to reinvent the wheel.

We have a lot of fragmentation as well—a lot of people doing the same thing in the same space with no real coordination because energetic individuals or existing church traditions have not recognized each other. For purposes of thinking through situations, or bringing to bear a Christian presence on things like the law, for example, the fragmentation and the desire for quick results, which in other ways is okay, has been a problem.

Recently I've been hearing in the news that the Supreme Court of the United States will have six Catholics and three Jews. Why no evangelical Protestants? Because, I think, as evangelical Protestants, we have spent our energies on doing things in a hurry, sometimes with very good results. We have not, however, spent our energies on doing the kind of careful, painstaking, slow, results-oriented type of training that leads to the production of first-rate lawyers who can reason in appropriate judicial ways in the various ways the Catholic and Jewish communities have sustained.

American evangelical Protestants eagerly exploit radio, television, and now the Internet as means to propagate the Christian faith. But these groups have done very little to think about the impact an intensively media-oriented society like ours has on the very shape of the Christian faith itself. Those are actually very important questions for us to consider in a society dominated by modern media.

Willard: With regard to "getting things done," what are your thoughts on this resurgence in social justice? Do you see a tie between the twentieth century fundamentalist/liberalist schism and this new vibrant face of U.S. Christianity?

Noll: Yes. I think that's putting your finger on something that's quite important right now. I do think that the more traditional or conservative Protestant groups in the U.S. retreated from public activity because of the fundamentalist/modernist crisis. It didn't have to be this way but traditional/conservative Christian groups thought that if you were active in social justice, social movements, it was automatically taking away from your loyalty to the historic Christian faith.

CHRISTIAN MINISTRY THAT MAJORS IN UNDERSTANDING CONTEMPORARY LIFE BUT IS WEAKER ON THE UNDERSTANDING OF SCRIPTURE IS NOT GOING TO BE MUCH HELP. IT WILL COMMUNICATE BUT HAVE LITTLE TO SAY.

That general pattern began to give way partly due to the stimulus of the Civil Rights Movement in the 1950s and '60s, coupled with the ability of Christian believers to mobilize against abortion in the 1970s. Since that time there's been a snowballing effect of more and more theologically conservative groups taking on the real interest in justice matters, and that is social development.

World Vision, for example, started with nothing in the mid-1950s and is now one of the largest international development organizations in the world. More recently, Gary Haugen's International Justice Mission has done a powerful job at broadcasting the need for concentrated Christian activity against sex trade trafficking throughout the world.

On the downside, however, I would say that the Christian strengths coming out of America are balanced by weaknesses that have to do with deeper broader analysis. And by that I mean there is not a whole lot of serious Christian reflection on, for example, commercial capitalism, or capitalism joined with the great advertising machine and modern media or even the recent war efforts in Iraq and Afghanistan.

Likewise, evangelicals miss opportunities like offering a well-informed theological analysis regarding our dependence on foreign oil in light of the recent Gulf of Mexico/BP oil well crisis. What about the problems with world trade and the funding of Islamic extremism that goes alongside our trade? Christian people in the U.S. more or less just go with the flow.

We're really good, I think, at seeing a cause and rapidly mobilizing to meet the problem. I don't think we're as good at thinking generally about the broader and deeper issues that sometimes surround the hot button causes that we can rally around.

Willard: Can you give some advice to the leaders as they engage in missions work and being the church in America?

Noll: I think that for church leaders of whatever age and whatever period in history the key thing is to be a bridge builder. And here I'm taking a metaphor that I've picked up from John Stott's great book on preaching. This image is one of communication that links together a strong understanding of the Scriptures—and I would add the church's thinking over time of the Scriptures. So, it's not just me studying the Scriptures, but it's my study of the Scriptures helped by the community of the faith that goes back in time and place.

The other end of the bridge is an understanding of the audiences to which the gospel is being proclaimed. So a very thorough and effective biblical understanding that's well-rooted in history and theology but does not understand contemporary life is not going to be particularly effective. Likewise, Christian ministry that majors in understanding contemporary life but is weaker on the understanding of Scripture is not going to be much help. It will communicate but have little to say.

The great strength of the bridge metaphor is to underscore that effective Christian communication always requires strong rooting in the Scriptures and Christian tradition, but then also has a strong empathy for the understanding of and engagement with the contemporary cultural situation. So, if Christians think together and work together they will be able to take more from the Scriptures and have a more effective understanding of the contemporary situation. ■

BEYOND
RELEVANCE

A COUNTERCULTURE FOR
THE COMMON GOOD

BY GABE LYONS

The red-lettered headline leapt off the black background of the April 4, 2009 *Newsweek* cover: "The Decline and Fall of Christian America." Based on sweeping new research, the story reported that the percentage of Americans claiming no religious identification has nearly doubled since 1990 and is now more evenly distributed across the United States. "While we remain a nation decisively shaped by religious faith," wrote *Newsweek* editor Jon Meacham, "our politics and our culture are, in the main, less influenced by movements and arguments of an explicitly Christian character than they were even five years ago."

Meacham isn't the only one to note that a perfect storm of change is brewing over America. Dozens of cultural observers have noted the American Christian movement's waning influence that is leaving our faith in an unforeseen moment. The tectonic plates of our culture have moved and are now resettling into a pluralistic, post-modern, post-Christian reality.

Some Christian cultural warriors are frustrated that political and cultural power is slipping from their fingers. Others are content to simply hang-on, hoping the return of Christ will come sooner rather than later. But, could the end of Christian America actually be good news for Christians? Could this moment become the stirrings of something beautiful? Is it possible to call "cease fire" in the culture war and still win the world?

A new generation of Christians says "yes." They see enormous opportunity despite the shifts happening in our world today. To a growing group of believers, this change represents a new chapter in the story God is telling through His people. It's a welcome change from the out-of-control manipulations they've experienced when religion gets intertwined too closely with public life. They see it as a new opportunity to send the gospel out in fresh and compelling ways.

BRAND NEW WORLD, SAME OLD QUESTION

Christian leaders of a new generation must once again wrestle with what Richard Niebuhr calls "the enduring problem," that is, the ongoing struggle to define the appropriate Christian response to culture. Every generation must face this quandary, and in our changing world, the conversation has been resurrected again. How should today's Christian relate to culture?

Separatism. In the past, some Christians fell into the separatist trap. They responded to culture with condemnation and retreat. Removing themselves as far away from the corruption of culture is the name of their game. But Christians who remove themselves from the world in hopes of self-preservation fail to realize that true cultural separation is impossible. More importantly, separation ignores the task we've been given to carry the love of God forward to those who might need it most.

Antagonism. Some Christians see little in the current culture worth redeeming and have decided to fight against almost everything culture promotes. Offended by our current cultural disposition, they want to flip over the tables of society instead of negotiating the difficult terrain of working it out from within. By default, they are known for being great at pointing out the problems of society, but they rarely offer good or practical solutions and alternatives that promote a better way of life. They succeed in stating clearly what they are *against*, but their Achilles heel is suggesting alternatives that embody what they are for.

Relevance. Others have gone to the opposite extreme by falling into the "relevance trap." In my estimation, this is probably the larger threat for Christian leaders today. In an effort to appeal to outsiders, some Christians simply copy culture. They become a Xerox of what they perceive as hip in hopes that people will perceive them—and their organizations, ministries, and churches—as "cool" and give them a chance. Unfortunately, this pursuit of pop-culture removes the church from its historically prophetic position in society. Relating to the world by following the world is a recipe for disaster.

A NEW GENERATION OF CHRISTIANS REALIZES THAT—LIKE SALT—WE CAN ONLY BE USEFUL WHEN WE ARE ACTIVE AND ENGAGED.

Separatism, antagonism, and relevance are all ineffective methods for social change, and recognizing this, a new generation of Christian leaders has adopted a new way of thinking about our world. These new leaders—I refer to them as "the next Christians"—are living in the tension of being prophetic with their lives while serving others and inviting them into a better way. The next Christians don't concern themselves with popularity, what they can achieve for themselves, or whether the masses are following. Instead, they are boldly leading out, and modeling a countercultural way of relating to society. Though it may sound like a new approach, it's actually quite old. But it's a promising key development for the future of Christian life in the West.

A COUNTERCULTURE FOR THE COMMON GOOD

Placing the label "countercultural" on the next Christians may seem odd to you. When I initially discovered this characteristic among the next leaders within our faith, it struck me as odd as well. The word *countercultural* conjures up images of a muddy Woodstock lawn, burning bras, gay rights activists, a lone voice on Tiananmen Square, anti-capitalist anarchists, white supremacist groups, and other anti-mainstream movements. With these sorts of visions in your head, the label wouldn't seem to fit. Yet it all makes sense once you understand the kind of counterculture they represent.

The next Christians recognize that sin has corrupted every aspect of our world, and they don't accept the belief that God is *only* concerned with saving individuals while our world spins out of control on its predestined path to destruction. In contrast, they hold on to Jesus' more robust vision: "You are the salt of the earth. But if the salt loses its saltiness, how can it be made salty again? It is no longer good for anything, except to be thrown out and trampled underfoot." (Matt. 5:13 TNIV)

A new generation of Christians realizes that—like salt—we can only be useful when we are active and engaged. They flee the temptations to either avoid the spoiling cultural meat of this world altogether or to become like the meat in order to attract more flies. Left on its own, even in proximity to meat, salt will do nothing to keep the meat from going bad. And meat left alone, without salt, will rot and be rendered useless. But when the two intermingle—like when salt is rubbed deep into a filet mignon—it not only preserves the steak but also expresses its greatest attributes in taste, quality, and flavor.

The next Christians see themselves as salt, preserving agents actively restoring in the middle of a decaying culture. They attach themselves to people and structures that are in danger of rotting while availing themselves to Christ's redeeming power to do work through them. They understand that by being restorers they fight against the cultural norms, to often flow counter to the cultural tide. But they feel that, as Christians, they've been called to partner with God in restoring and renewing everything they see falling apart. Their commitment to hold back evil, to repair systems and structures, and to heal people who are broken and suffering from the fall gives an alternative trajectory to the average life.

Paradoxically, in our current cultural context, this not only opens up more people to personal salvation, but it also sustains a God-glorifying testimony to the world of His restoration power at work. It is truly *good news* to the world. Rather than fighting *off* cul-

ture to protect an insular Christian community, they are fighting *for* the world to redeem it. This is the essence of being what pastor Tim Keller refers to as "a counterculture for the common good."

One riveting example can be found in Portland, Oregon. This Western metropolis is a proudly liberal place known as one of the most unchurched cities in North America. I've known that leaders in Portland have been praying and working together for years on various projects that affect their city, but now the tremors have reached the surface.

THE CITY OF PORTLAND WILL HOST THE Q GATHERING APRIL 27-29, 2011.

FOR MORE INFORMATION, GO TO WWW.QIDEAS.ORG.

Enter world evangelist Luis Palau and his son, Kevin. On behalf of several hundred churches, they met with Portland's mayor to ask a simple question: "How can we serve for the good of the city— no strings attached?" Local pastors and Christian leaders wanted to repair the church's storied relationship with the community and were taking seriously Jeremiah's challenge to "Seek the peace and prosperity of the city to which I have carried you." (Jer. 29:7 TNIV)

Five areas were identified for further exploration: homelessness, hunger/poverty, health/wellness, public schools, and the environment. The agenda was clear and concise, and the church responded.

Portland's small but committed Christian community caught a vision for their city and began to raise up volunteers. "Season of Service" was born, and within the first year, 450 congregations and 28,000 individuals were enlisted in the cause. They established a dozen free medical/dental clinics to serve the area's uninsured and launched Home Again Mentoring Plan, a program providing long-term mentor teams for homeless families. Portland was so impressed with the work being done, they even allowed churches to begin "adopting" public schools. In a city where the Christian community had little influence, churches are now seen as a powerful force for lasting change.

RATHER THAN RETREAT INTO THEIR CHURCHES AND CONDUCT BUSINESS AS USUAL, THESE RESTORATION-MINDED CHRISTIANS ENGAGED THEIR CITY AS THE COUNTERCULTURAL HANDS AND FEET OF JESUS CHRIST.

Portland's mayor Sam Adams—the first openly gay mayor of a major U.S. city—has publicly praised the initiative and offered his full support for three consecutive years. As he issued the official declaration for Season of Service '09 in front of five hundred pastors, he gratefully explained, "When we first heard the idea … we were skeptical, but our modest hopes were incredibly exceeded by what you and your churches accomplished."

During that same meeting, leaders representing more than three hundred churches presented the mayor with a gift of $100,000 to help reduce the high school dropout rate and mentor those in homeless families.

While some churches may have used that money to launch a building campaign or start a new program, these churches gave it away.

The media has taken notice as well. An editorial in *USA Today* praised the "stereotype-busting sub-plots … the most intriguing of all being the way the Seasons of Service has thrust the area's Evangelicals into partnership with the city's most liberal leaders." *Willamette Week*—Portland's alternative newspaper—surprisingly noted that the church community "has moved its unashamedly evangelical operations into the most secular of cities with nary a peep of protest." Even *Reader's Digest* listed Season of Service in their Best of 2009 issue, naming it one of the nation's best community service initiatives.

The people of Portland are being refreshed by a new experience with Christianity. Rather than retreat into their churches and conduct business as usual, these restoration-minded Christians engaged their city as the countercultural hands and feet of Jesus Christ. Over time, the church has earned a seat at the table. They are included on serious discussions about the future of Portland and illustrate well the difference a countercultural community for the common good can make on the place they call home.

This is the shape of Christian cultural engagement in our new era. As Keller reminds us, "Christianity will not be attractive enough to win influence except through sacrificial service to all people, regardless of their beliefs." The next Christians try to create the most good for all people, regardless of race, class, or religion. They don't strive for what's best only in their own community of believers, though that's important. They concentrate on the common good—those things which are of benefit to all people in God's creation.

A BETTER WAY FORWARD

Just as the cultural presumption of a Christian America begins to fade away, a new breed of Christians are peeking over the cultural horizon. Their refreshing, authentic lives don't just fill a void of Christian inactivity, they replace the negative perceptions that had somehow become the only image of Christianity many in our society had experienced.

A commitment to being countercultural rather than being removed or "relevant" isn't always easy. Living differently can be hard. Going against the ebbs and flows of culture can create friction and sometimes provoke a hostile reaction to the good we are trying to create. Theologians Stanley Hauerwas and Will Willimon remind us that this should be expected, for "whenever a people are bound together in loyalty to a story that includes something as strange as the Sermon on the Mount, we are put at odds with the world."

Yet, it is through maintaining this cultural orientation that the world can experience God's restoration power and people will be convinced that our faith is all we claim, all that Jesus commissioned His followers to. As the apostle Peter encourages, "Live such good lives among the pagans that, though they accuse you of doing wrong, they may see your good deeds and glorify God on the day he visits us." (1 Pet. 2:12 TNIV)

Is a countercultural community the answer to restoring the soul of the world, winning the skeptics, and revitalizing our faith? We'll have to wait and see. For now we know that the clear call of Jesus is for the Christian community to be salt on a rotting world and light in the dimmest places. Not simply a bunch of small lights in all the dark corners of the world, but a communal light that provides a picture to the world of what a loving, sacrificial, countercultural community really is—a collective of people living by a different standard, raising the bar and inviting others to join us. In this way and others, the end of Christian America is truly good news for Christians. **C**

ESS

AN INTERVIEW WITH TAD AGOGLIA

BY TIMOTHY WILLARD

Hurricane Katrina changed the way our nation views and responds to national disasters. The people of New Orleans and the surrounding area still wince when they hear the weather reports for the hurricane season. The city continues to rebuild because of the devastation brought on by Katrina. The years following the great disaster forced many to redefine their way of life and their outlook on life. The storm washed away much of the city but the rebuilding process offered a chance to redefine itself, to start fresh.

Tad Agoglia worked cleanup after Katrina. He was rewarded with a lucrative contract and was able to build a solid team to respond to the needs at hand. But the impact of Katrina went deeper for Tad—far deeper than scoring sizable government contracts to clean up after natural disasters. The human element of the disaster deeply impacted Tad.

"What we saw with Katrina, as with all natural disasters," explains Tad, "is that several days can pass before local authorities or federal agencies can begin to assess the damage and start the daunting tasks of restoring order and establishing rescue and recovery operations. These first few days are critical; people in desperate need are left stranded—alone and in danger."

This reality moved Tad to action. He began to imagine what it would look like if someone—a team of people—

took it upon themselves to respond to natural disasters; those untamed events that can change a person's life, a community's identity, and a nation's morale within minutes. He imagined situations where major search and rescue efforts could be tackled along with clearing roads for other first responders to get to the scene. He imagined a fleet of state-of-the-art trucks and equipment uniquely designed to handle the worst of conditions. And he imagined doing all this at no cost to the public.

PIPE DREAM? NOT HARDLY.

Tad took his imagination, his willpower, and his entire savings account and set them into motion. In May 2007 Tad assembled his team, the genesis of a national first response team for natural disasters: The First Response Team of America (FRTA).

He and his crews identify and access disaster sites throughout the United States, bringing help and hope to all those in need. They use heavy equipment and some of the most advanced technology available for search and rescue. Since Tad and his team are nomadic—always moving from one disaster site to the next—they can act with speed and precision. And, when they arrive on the scene, they bring overwhelming support.

"Having the proper gear is just as important as getting to a disaster site swiftly," Tad says. "My crews are able to use cameras and audio devices that allow them to go through rubble looking for people who are pinned, people who depend on a rapid response." They plan for it all. Darkness can often impede rescue efforts, but FRTA uses light towers that can illuminate up to eight acres at a time so search and rescue can continue while looters are kept at bay.

Tad's crew sound a bit like a supercharged G.I. Joe squad specializing in bringing hope to decimated communities. But what did it take for Tad to get this highly mobile force of hope up and running?

TAKING A RISK

When Tad first came up with the idea to build a first response team for natural disasters and to self-fund the entire operation, people thought he'd lost it. And, to some extent, Tad had to convince himself: Was it really worth it? Was it entrepreneurial suicide to take a company he had created to make money and turn it into a completely free service company?

"Relief companies basically profit off of people's misfortune," admits Tad. "It's just how the business side of disaster relief works. Companies land major contracts three months after the disaster and *then* go in to clean up. But, for me, something was not right with that scenario." The business side of it all, however, did not blind Tad to a major problem in the disaster relief timeline that he felt needed to be addressed. "People need help immediately and that's what First Response Team addresses. We don't have to wait three months to take action. We're not bound by bureaucracy. We can actually make an immediate impact in the lives of the victims."

There was a void in the disaster relief world and Tad had found a way to fill it. But then there's the actual *doing* involved with creating a new type of business. Tad's idea demanded the use of specialized heavy equipment, well-paid manual labor, and the flexibility to go anywhere at any time, no matter what. "I could have gone to Washington and lobbied for funding and spent years raising enough money to get up and running. That wasn't an option for me. I decided to put my money where my dreams were and take a bit of a leap."

Tad likens himself to a high-stakes poker player. And the comparison fits. He recently met Phil Hellmuth, World Series of Poker legend, at a charity event. After spending some time together Tad realized how similar they were. "Phil bets a lot of money which carries a high yield of cash. I risk a major investment on equipment and even my life (and the lives of my crew), which yields hope for hurting people—helping save and influence lives." It's a high stakes game that Tad plays day in and day out. But the rewards far outweigh the risks.

When asked about what he thinks is lacking in modern day leadership Tad gave a simple reply. "Too many people allow fear to dictate their lives. To lead is to risk."

Sure, there were plenty of naysayers along the path for Tad and his vision. But they don't phase him. In fact, whereas some leaders like to keep contrary people around as a way to keep sharp, Tad goes the other way. "I don't have time for people who want to sit around and complain or discuss what we should be doing. I just want to do it." Pastor Chuck Swindoll once said that a leader is someone oft misunderstood yet still pursues what he's supposed to do.

IN THESE DARKEST HOURS,
THE FIRST RESPONSE TEAM
OF AMERICA IS THERE, FREE
OF CHARGE, ARMED WITH
SPECIALIZED EQUIPMENT,
ADVANCED COMMUNICATION
SYSTEMS, AND A COMMITMENT
TO SAVE LIVES AND RESTORE
HOPE, SIMPLY BECAUSE IT'S
THE RIGHT THING TO DO.

Tad was misunderstood at first. Now he's impacting government officials, local communities, and individuals who face dire circumstances.

A LEADER'S LOT

The First Response Team of America has to be able to show up anywhere in the country at any time when disaster strikes. However impressive the outfit looks or whatever the impact it is having in communities all over the country is a direct result of one leader counting the cost and stepping headlong into risk. We often hear leaders speak of taking a leap of faith—passion wins out. But for Tad, it is a balance of planning and passion.

There is an inherent cost involved in any endeavor. Even the greatest teacher ever, Jesus, talked about considering the costs of building a house before beginning. When we get an idea or feel called to a certain project or task we need to consider the cost. There's no substitute for being diligent in our planning and scheming.

"After I made a plan to create this company," explains Tad, "I then had to confront the risk part of it. Will it work? How will I pay for it? I didn't have all the answers. But I had a peace about what I had to do. It's not up to us to succeed at everything we are called to do. But it is up to us to heed the call and *do* something about it."

This is the lot of all leaders: understand the unique call to do something, figure out how to do it great, and do it with everything you have in you.

Too often leaders believe they have a divine calling and just think God will do all the work. Without giving the idea deep thought and consideration they begin something on passion alone—calling others to cling to their vision. But the organizations that succeed are the ones that go through great pains to discern the need and then figure out the best way to address it. "We aren't just called to have great ideas," says Tad. "We're called to take great ideas and mold them into an outstanding reality. And this takes work and tons of risk and a lot of sleepless nights."

A FEARLESS THOUGHT

One of the strong themes running through Tad's line of work is the idea that every day is a gift. "You never know when you're going to run into *the* storm. The one that takes you home," explains Tad. "If there's one thing I've learned it's that every day is a gift. We see people who've lost family members in storms as well as all their earthly possessions. We are never promised tomorrow—this is a real life fact I see every day. So what are we *doing now* to make today special?"

But so many in our culture are content to stand on the sidelines, offering critique but never solutions to problems that ail our society. Tad says that this kind of behavior cheapens life. It's not only about talking through problems; it's about finding solutions, it's about *being* the solution. Tad is passionate about people finding something to do and latching on to it. He loves to see people in their sweet spot pouring themselves into their dreams. "That's what life's all about."

Nobody wants to wake up someday and find themselves on their death bed with a fist full of regrets. "Who wants to look back on their life and be saddened by the fact that they failed to act when given the chance?" Tad's question applies to each of us. Our country continues to struggle through one of the worst financial times in memory. There is great opportunity for risk-takers bent on making the world a better place. There is great opportunity for leaders to step past the negativity of others and decide to make a difference.

Tad explained that the one thing on his heart recently was a question: What is it like to be fearless? When we look at Tad's example of leadership, we find that it's not that he acted without fear. That isn't fearlessness. It's that he acted in spite of fear. So maybe being fearless is less about operating with no fear and more about seeing the fear—confronting the fear—and stepping forth in a grand effort to overcome.

Tad and his crew stare fear in the face every day. They see it in the faces of the victims they rescue. They see it in the faces of community and national officials who don't have answers. He sees it swirling in the very storms that ransack and destroy. Yet, in all the fear, in all the uncertainty, Tad found a way to lead where no one was leading. He found a way to step out and do what was in his heart: help and show compassion to those hurting.

Tad's answer to fear? Big trucks, crazy tractors, and cool hovercrafts. **C**

NOBODY WANTS TO WAKE UP SOMEDAY AND FIND THEMSELVES ON THEIR DEATH BED WITH A FIST FULL OF REGRETS. "WHO WANTS TO LOOK BACK ON THEIR LIFE AND BE SADDENED BY THE FACT THAT THEY FAILED TO ACT WHEN GIVEN THE CHANCE?" TAD'S QUESTION APPLIES TO EACH OF US.

SEEK IT LIKE SILVER

THE TENSION BETWEEN THINKING, FEELING & DOING

BY JOHN PIPER

THE MOVE OF '79

All my life I have lived with the tension between thinking and feeling and doing.

After twenty-two years of non-stop formal education and six years of college teaching, I left academia for the pastorate at age thirty-four. That was almost thirty years ago. I remember the night of October 14, 1979, when I wrote seven pages in my journal about the crisis in my soul concerning college teaching versus pastoral ministry. It was one of the most important days of my life—I can see that now.

It seemed to me then that these things—thinking and feeling and doing—would perhaps find a better balance in the church than in school. By "better" I mean a balance that would fit my gifts, and God's call, and people's needs, and the purposes of God for this world. I think I did the right thing. But I don't mean it would be right for everybody.

I firmly believe in and want to celebrate the indispensable place of education in the cause of Christ. If every faculty member in the university or seminary did what I did, it would be tragic. I love what God did for me in academia for twenty-eight years, from ages six to thirty-four.

I am not among the number who looks back with dismay on what I was or wasn't taught. If I had it to do over again, I would take almost all the same classes with the same teachers and teach almost all the same classes. I didn't expect college and seminary and graduate school to teach me things that have to be learned on the job. If I have stumbled, it wasn't their fault.

THE PAINFUL JOY OF ACADEMIA

Nor did I leave academia because it was spiritually stifling. On the contrary. All through college, and more so through seminary, and then even more in my six years of college teaching, my reading and thinking and writing made my heart burn with zeal for God. I have never been one of those who found the heart shrivel as God and his Word are known better. Putting more knowledge in my head about God and his ways was like throwing wood in the furnace of my worship. For me, seeing has meant savoring. And the clearer the seeing, the sweeter the savoring.

Not that there weren't tears. Some of my notions about God went up in the flames of biblical truth. It hurt. I would put my face in my hands some afternoons and weep with the pain of confusion. But, as the Native American proverb says, the soul would have no rainbow if the eye had no tears. Some joys are only possible on the other side of sorrow. It is true when the preacher says, "In much wisdom is much vexation, and he who increases knowledge increases sorrow." (Eccles. 1:18 ESV) But it is worth it.

And I don't mean that the seeing which led to savoring was easy. The work involved in figuring out what the Bible means when it talks about God is often agonizingly difficult. I know something of Luther's agonizing statement, "I beat importunately upon Paul at that place, most ardently desiring to know what St. Paul wanted."[1] I simply mean that when all is said and done, the work of thinking led me again and again to worship. Academia was life-giving for me.

INFLAMED TO PREACH BY ROMANS 9

I left in search of a new life of exultation over the truth. There is an irony in the fact that what led to my leaving was a sabbatical in which I wrote a book on Romans 9.[2] *The Justification of God* is the most complicated, intellectually demanding book I have ever written. It deals with the most difficult theological issues and one of the hardest texts in the Bible. Yet, ironically, the research

and writing of this book was what God used to inflame my heart for preaching and pastoral ministry. Writing this most difficult book about God's sovereignty was not dispiriting; it was incendiary. This was the God I wanted more than anything to proclaim—not just explain.

Yet it was the explaining that set fire to the proclaiming. I have not forgotten that. I haven't forgotten because it is still true. "As I mused," says the psalmist, "the fire burned; then I spoke with my tongue." (Ps. 39:3 ESV) Musing. Brooding. Pondering. Thinking. That has been for me the pathway to seeing and savoring and singing and speaking—and staying. Year after year, this has been my work—prayer-saturated, Spirit-dependent thinking about what God has revealed of himself to provide fuel for passion and preaching.

Thinking is indispensable on the path to passion for God. Thinking is not an end in itself. Nothing but God himself is finally an end in itself. Thinking is not the goal of life. Thinking, like non-thinking, can be the ground for boasting. Thinking, without prayer, without the Holy Spirit, without obedience, without love, will puff up and destroy. (1 Cor. 8:1) But thinking under the mighty hand of God, thinking soaked in prayer, thinking carried by the Holy Spirit, thinking tethered to the Bible, thinking in pursuit of more reasons to praise and proclaim the glories of God, thinking in the service of love—such thinking is indispensable in a life of fullest praise to God.

A TOUGH TENSION AND THE LAMENT
OF THE THINKERS

And yet the tension remains. Thinking and feeling and doing jostle each other in my life, jockeying for more room. There never seems to be a satisfactory proportion. Should I be doing more, thinking more, feeling more, expressing more feeling? No doubt this discomfort is owed partly to quirks in my personality, factors in my background, and the remaining corruption in my heart.

But this tension is also due to a history of over-intellectualism and anti-intellectualism in the church; and it is due partly to a complexity in the Bible itself. Too often, the church has been ambivalent about "the life of the mind." America, in particular, has a long history of evangelical suspicion of education and intellectual labor. The most notable narration of this story for evangelicals is Mark Noll's *The Scandal of the Evangelical Mind*, whose first

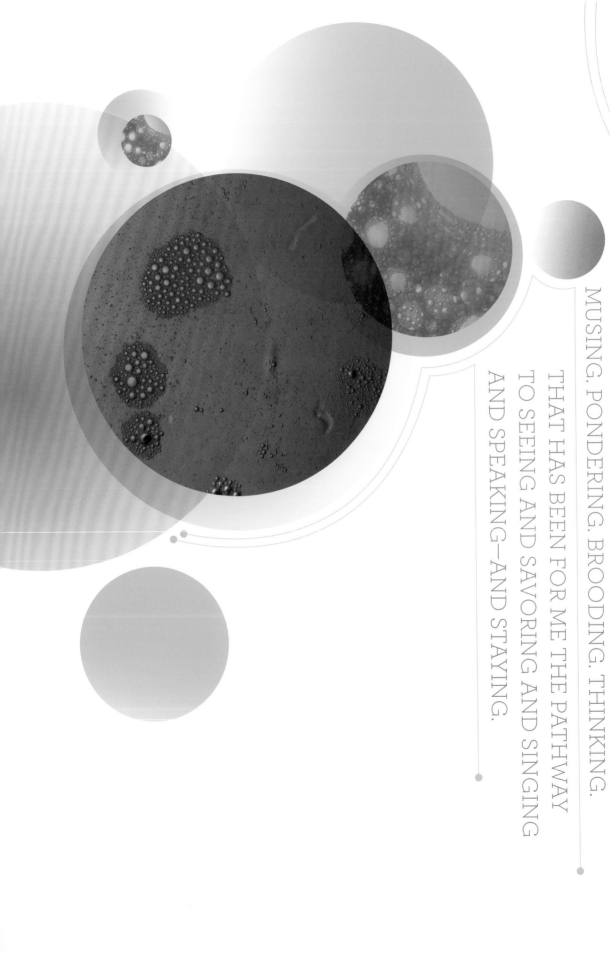

MUSING. PONDERING. BROODING. THINKING.
THAT HAS BEEN FOR ME THE PATHWAY
TO SEEING AND SAVORING AND SINGING
AND SPEAKING—AND STAYING.

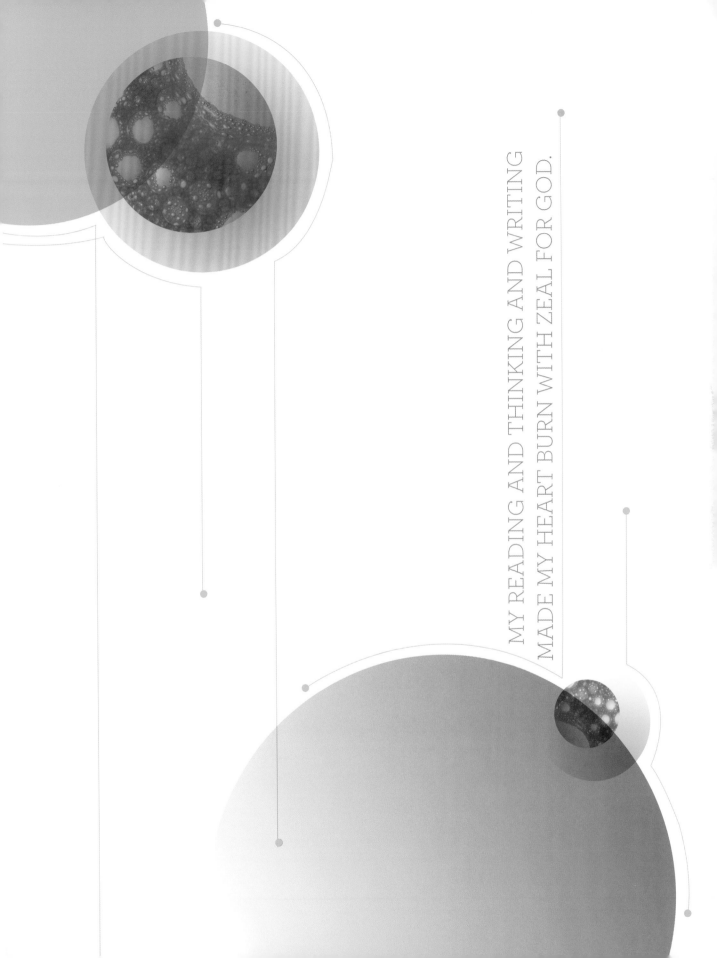

MY READING AND THINKING AND WRITING MADE MY HEART BURN WITH ZEAL FOR GOD.

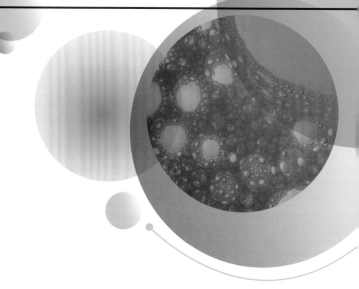

sentence is, "The scandal of the evangelical mind is that there is not much of an evangelical mind."[3]

Thirty years before Noll's indictment Harry Blamires wrote, "In contradistinction to the secular mind, no vital Christian mind plays fruitfully, as a coherent and recognizable influence, upon our social, political, or cultural life. ... There is no Christian mind."[4] And since Noll, others have joined the lament. J. P. Moreland has a chapter called, "How We Lost the Christian Mind and Why We Must Recover It."[5] And Os Guinness has written *Fit Bodies Fat Minds: Why Evangelicals Don't Think and What to Do About It.*[6]

These friends are describing not just the world but the home I grew up in. As far as the world goes, R. C. Sproul has written that "we live in what may be the most anti-intellectual period in the history of Western civilization."[7] As far as my fundamentalist upbringing goes, Noll says that for the kind of thinking that embraces society, the arts, the human person, and nature—"for that kind of thinking the habits of mind fundamentalism encouraged can only be called a disaster."[8] It is not surprising perhaps then that I find myself pulled in different directions. For even Noll admits that there are amazing accomplishments for the good of the world brought about by the very impulses which, in part, undermined the deeper life of the mind.[9]

KNOWLEDGE: DANGEROUS AND LIBERATING

But whatever I inherited in the atmosphere of my world and my home, the more mature tension I experience between thinking and feeling and doing is due largely to the Bible itself. There are some sentences in God's Word that make knowledge sound dangerous and others that make it sound glorious. For example, on the one hand, it says, "Knowledge puffs up, but love builds up" (1 Cor. 8:1 NET); and, on the other hand, it says, "You will know the truth, and the truth will set you free." (John 8:32 ESV) Knowing is dangerous. Knowing is liberating. And that is not an isolated paradox.

So what I want to do is take you with me into the Bible itself to see how God has ordered this act of thinking in relation to other crucial acts in life. How does it relate to our believing, and worshiping, and living in this world? Why are there so many warnings about "knowledge" (1 Tim. 6:20), and "the wisdom of this world" (1 Cor. 3:19),

and "philosophy" (Col. 2:8), and the "debased mind" (Rom. 1:28), and "the wise and understanding" who can't see (Luke 10:21), and those whose understanding is darkened? (Eph. 4:18)

THINK OVER WHAT I SAY

In spite of all these warnings, the overwhelming message of the Bible is that knowing the truth is crucial. And thinking—eagerly and humbly using the mind God gave us, and using it well—is essential to knowing the truth.

Two passages of Scripture provide my main point. The first is 2 Timothy 2:7, where Paul says to Timothy, "Think over what I say, for the Lord will give you understanding in everything." The command is that Timothy should think, consider, use his mind to try to understand what Paul means. And the reason Paul gives for this thinking is this: "For the Lord will give you understanding." Paul does not put these in tension: thinking on the one side and receiving the gift of understanding from God on the other side. They go together. Thinking is essential on the path to understanding. But understanding is a gift of God.

SEEK IT LIKE SILVER

The other passage is Proverbs 2:1–6. I'll boil it down to two verses to make it easier to see how similar it is to 2 Timothy 2:7. "If you ... raise your voice for understanding, if you seek it like silver ... then you will ... find the knowledge of God. For the Lord gives wisdom; from his mouth come knowledge and understanding." The point is that we should seek understanding like a

THINKING IS INDISPENSABLE ON THE PATH TO PASSION FOR GOD. BUT UNDERSTANDING IS A GIFT OF GOD.

miser seeks silver. We should use our minds with eagerness and skill. What is the reason given? The same one Paul gave: "For the Lord gives wisdom." They go together—our seeking understanding and God's giving it. Seeking it like silver is essential to finding. But finding is a gift of God.

A story about Benjamin Warfield may make the point clear. Warfield taught at Princeton Seminary for thirty-four years until his death in 1921. He reacted with dismay toward those who saw opposition between prayer for divine illumination and rigorous thinking about God's written Word. In 1911 he gave an address to students with this exhortation:

"Sometimes we hear it said that ten minutes on your knees will give you a truer, deeper, more operative knowledge of God than ten hours over your books. 'What!' is the appropriate response, 'than ten hours over your books, on your knees?'"[10]

Both-and. Not either-or. That's the vision I am trying to encourage you with. **C**

THAT'S HOT!

HOW THE CHRISTIAN FAITH SUFFERS IN A CELEBRITY WORLD

BY TIMOTHY WILLARD & JASON LOCY

PHOTO CREDITS: Nicolas Genin, Eneaus De Troya, University Unions Technology and Design, Keithe Hinkle, Rubenstein, Keith Allison, Patrik Ottosson and John Venderhaagen.

"That's Hot!" It was the catchphrase of the 2000s. Like "Gee Wally" and "Whatchoo talkin' 'bout Willis?" and "Did I do that?" that came before. Coined by the blond socialite Paris Hilton on her reality TV show *The Simple Life*, the phrase became the oft-repeated staple of office one-liners. The jet-setting airhead-heiress to the Hilton Hotel fortune had never worked a day in her life. Her over-the-top spending and partying made her a household name and landed her the reality show where the phrase would crash its way into our lexicon.

Paris' grandfather built a hotel empire and now she is the lucky recipient of his good fortune. The media can't resist telling the wild stories of how Paris handles her wealth. She is a pop-culture icon. According to Daniel Boorstin's definition, Paris is the quintessential modern celebrity: "A person known for [their] well-knowness."[1]

We consume the lives of those on the screen, we invite them into our homes through television and DVDs, and so we expect, and want, to know more about them. Madonna and her baby. Tom Cruise and his couch jumping. Mel Gibson and his yelling. Paris Hilton and her sex making. All front page news stories. At some point we start paying less attention to their talents, if they have them, and more attention to their "real" lives.

They may be introduced to us through a movie role but at some point their real life becomes more interesting than their on-screen roles. Their acting or songwriting or athleticism are no longer the real story; instead it is their life that we want to know about. Like a never-ending soap opera we watch the celebrity-life day in and day out, wondering what will happen next. Who will she date next? Are they back on drugs? Did he cheat on his girlfriend?

Neal Gabler, in his book *Life: The Movie*, takes Boorstin's definition of celebrity further. Gabler writes, "Movies had stars. Life had celebrities."[2] Celebrity is not about being famous, it is about having a life story that the public is watching.

MY APHRODITE

The "King of Pop." Michael Jackson, dead at age 50. It was one of the biggest news events of 2009. The week he died, reports highlighting his legacy were the leading news stories in the country. The coverage received more air time from the major news outlets than a U.S. withdrawal from Iraq, the Afghan war, the governor of California declaring an economic emergency, and Sarah Palin stepping down as governor of Alaska, all of which happened during the same week. When Elvis Presley died in 1977 it wasn't even the lead story on the *CBS Evening News with Walter Cronkite*. On the day of Jackson's death, CNN had a 900% spike in viewership.[3]

Despite not having released an album in eight years, Jackson remained in the public eye. He began to be known more for his skin bleaching and marriages and lawsuits and holding babies over balconies and inviting young boys to his bed, and less for his music. A celebrity. But his celebrity status, it seems, was bigger than the others. This celebrity was one we idolized.

When we "call on god, and god is dead,"[4] man creates his own. Unsure of the real God, unsure of how He plays into our success and happiness and everyday lives, we call on the gods of society—inventing as many as we can. The Greeks had Zeus and Aphrodite and Poseidon. Today we have Michael Jackson and Princess Di and Madonna. They are images *made by man's design and skill*. (See Acts 17:24-34 ESV)

But no matter how hard we try, an idol cannot fulfill man's need for God—a real, living, intimate God. We need our God to be accessible, not with the on/off button of a remote control but through relationship. Klaus Bockmuehl puts it this way: "An idol leads a man, by necessity, into loneliness. An idol leads man into loneliness, when what man needs is a god with whom he can have dialogue."[5] The God of Abraham does not, however, lead anyone into loneliness. He leads people into Himself.

CELEBRITY ME

The allure of fame, however, is too overwhelming for us, the pull of culture too great. Our desire to lead a celebrity life, coupled with the search for success that the world presents, leads us to our own scripted realities. We think of ourselves as stars in our own drama. In his book *Empire of Illusion*, author Christopher Hedges writes, "We try to see ourselves moving through our life as a camera would see us. … We invent movies that play inside our heads. We imagine ourselves the main characters. We imagine how an audience would react to each event in the movie of our life."[6]

We become real to ourselves by being seen by others. It validates us. In our effort to be known we wield the powerful shield of the computer to become who we want to be.

"Meet Julia Allison. She can't act. She can't sing. She's not rich. But thanks to a genius for self-promotion—plus Flickr, Twitter, and her blogs—she's become an Internet celebrity. How she did it—and how you can too."[7] This was the subtitle for *Wired* magazine's feature article about Julia Allison. Julia graced the cover in her sexed-up style with an equally provocative article layout conveying the idea that she is a celebrity. But is she really? What are the qualifications that make her a celebrity?

Julia represents an extreme example of veneer. She is a fabricated expression of her true self. Through constant blogging and Twittering she has leveraged the Internet and created a persona whose sole purpose is to be a celebrity. "Her trick, she says, is to think of herself as the subject of a magazine profile, with every post or update adding dimensions to her as a character. 'I treat it like a fire, … You have to add logs, or it'll be like one of those YouTube videos that flame out.'"[8]

Because of people—quasi-celebrities—like Julia Allison, who achieve celebrity status through personality inflation, celebrity is open game to anyone with a laptop and web camera. We can all fabricate publicity stunts and manipulate pictures to become someone we are not. Everyone is entitled to his or her 15 minutes—or 15MB—of fame.

In the pursuit of self we find ourselves moving further from God. We see Him fade away as the star of self shines bright. "Something has stepped between our existence and God to shut off the light of heaven ... [and] that something is in fact ourselves, our own bloated selfhood."[9]

Celebrity Me.

THE DREAD SPIRIT

After Jesus was baptized we find Him alone in the wilderness. For 40 days He fasted and prayed. Alone and hungry, He was tempted with the same things that get at us today in the celebrity world. "The wise and dread spirit"[10] tempted Jesus with wealth and celebrity and glory.

Physically, the thing Jesus must have wanted most was food. And so, this is where the tempter starts. "You are the Son of God. Turn that stone into bread," said the dread spirit. And, with the point of a finger or flicker of a thought, Jesus could have turned the stone to bread. It would have been no big deal. After all, later in His life, He would turn water to wine and feed the 5,000 with the lunch of a boy.

But Jesus didn't need the bread. He didn't need what the tempter thought He needed. "Man does not live on bread alone," He said. The world thinks we need abundance. It thinks we need wealth. Success. But no matter what the bread of society looks like, Jesus says, "No, thanks." Our sustenance is found in God.

The tempter came back with another test. "Throw Yourself off this cliff. Call on the angels, they can save You." If Jesus were to dive off the cliff and if angels were to save Him, the story of His grand escape would spread quickly. Jesus would become an instant celebrity. He would be loved and revered and worshiped. Certainly, He could skip the whole messy business of the crucifixion.

But we see Jesus shun the spotlight. "Don't test God," He said. Jesus didn't need the fame of celebrity. He needed to be in the work of the Father. And, in the work of the Father, there is no need to seek celebrity.

The tempter, a persistent bugger, returns a third time. This time Jesus is shown all the kingdoms of the land and their splendor. "All of this," he says, "I will give you." All Jesus had to do was deny Himself and He would have wealth, fame, power. But Jesus didn't need a shortcut to glory. He didn't need the quick fix. And so, Jesus looked at His tempter and said, "Get away from Me. I serve God alone."

And that was that. Jesus was left alone. The temptation He faced during those 40 days shows us that man is not meant to live chasing after wealth or fame or glory. That path is a never-ending pursuit—one that fades, one that is hollow.[11]

THE VISIBLE MUST REMAIN HIDDEN

As Jesus' life unfolds we see a stark contrast to the celebrity culture. The Kingdom culture elevates the greatness of Christ and the service to others. Jesus shows us that those who follow Him are not called to seek visibility but anonymity, giving the glory to the Creator.

As Christians, we don't and shouldn't seek to be known; instead, we are to seek the good of others. Dietrich Bonhoeffer, in *The Cost of Discipleship*, presents the question, "How do the disciples [of Jesus] differ from the heathen? What does it really mean to be a Christian?"[12] He answers this with the word *perissos*—extraordinary. But His extraordinary is not how we would normally define it. Used in Matthew 5:47, the word calls for the Christian to go beyond what is expected in the culture. It is a term of differentiation, a term for uncommon living.

If it is expected that we elevate ourselves in order to achieve some sort of fame or make more money, then to be *extraordinary*, according to Bonhoeffer, means that we seek that which is uncommon in our society— greed gives way to generosity. We lift up others instead of self.

To be extraordinary in our faith is being the light that shines before the world. Bonhoeffer reminds us that it's not that we *have* light; we *are* the light. We are,

IN OUR BROKENNESS THE
CELEBRITY MOTIVE COMPELS US
TO BE KNOWN. IN OUR HUMILITY
THE CHRISTIAN MOTIVE COMPELS
US TO BE HIDDEN—IN CHRIST.

therefore, visible to the world. Bonhoeffer continues, "The better righteousness [that which is extraordinary] of the disciples must have a motive which lies beyond self. Of course it has to be visible, but they must take care that it does not become visible simply for the sake of becoming visible."[13] Our care is not in fame, it is to know God. All else is advertising.

So it comes to motive. In our brokenness the celebrity motive compels us to be known. In our humility the Christian motive compels us to be hidden—in Christ. When we attempt to communicate like the world, be cool like the world, use the same devices to become popular, are we being extraordinary? Or are we merely rising to the world's standard that goes no further than self-glorification? "That which is visible must also be hidden."[14]

We must be so focused on Christ that the wake of our light is unknown to us. Our intentions cannot be to gain influence or become great.

Our narrative plays out before Christ, not man. It is not a celebrity narrative of fame and fortune but one of humility, giving, sacrifice, unselfishness, and honesty. In this realization we begin to find our way. We begin to see that, compared to the spectacle of celebrity, our life is otherworldly. Extraordinary. ◼

A KINGDOM VIEW

BY DALLAS WILLARD

What is the central message of the church? There are many dimensions to the church and, arguably, plenty of problems that need to be addressed. But, for various reasons, the church's main problem is with its central message and the inability to make sense with what Jesus Himself presented as the central message. Jesus' message undermines all of the efforts of the church. Unless you understand that Jesus invites us, through faith in Him, to actually live *in* the Kingdom of God now there will not be a basis for discipleship and transformation.

Living in the Kingdom now is another way to say *gospel living*—it's how to get into heaven *before you die*. That's why the New Testament routinely treats you as if you have already died because you have made a transition from a life on your own to a life that God Himself is living in His Kingdom.

So, you get to be a part of that Kingdom now. Jesus preached about the availability of the Kingdom of God to everyone; wherever they were and whoever they were. He announces the Kingdom and by His own presence makes it available. Once you get that idea, you can read the gospel and say, "Hey, that's what's happening."

The reality and effects of the Kingdom is God in action. He acts through all His instrumentalities. But the main thing to understand is God acts in relationship with us. We can call that the presence of God with us, the Holy Spirit, the power of the Word—but the important thing to understand is the Kingdom of God is God in action.

The concept of *God in action* turns out to be exactly the same thing as grace. So, grace now becomes a part of our lives, and we experience it by faith. We have to learn how to do this because we're usually in charge of what's happening, and we have to learn how to turn loose of that and how to live with God being in charge. And we can do that.

But grace does not *only* mean forgiveness. With grace you find almost immediately that it is for life, not for forgiveness. It's for enabling us to *live* in such a way that God is a part of our lives and is helping us to lead the life that He wants for us. The sinner is not the one who uses a lot of grace. It is, rather, the saint who uses more grace. The saint burns grace like a 747 burns fuel on takeoff because everything they do is a manifestation of grace. We're not running out of grace.

We have to learn how to do that, and it no longer means we just trust our own efforts to manage our lives—that's our kingdom. And, unfortunately, it turns out to be part of a darker kingdom. And when, as Colossians 1 says, we are translated out of the kingdom of darkness into the Kingdom of the Son of His love—we experience the new birth. Only then do we begin to experience grace for the first time. ◼

QUESTIONS FOR GROUP STUDY

YOU'RE A RACIST, YOU KNOW
Timothy Keller, page 28

In this column, Tim Keller states, "We began to see how, in so many ways, we made our cultural biases into moral principles and then judged people of other races as being inferior." Do you agree with this statement? Can you see evidence of the same in your own life? Discuss.

WHY CHRISTIANS SHOULD REJECT POP-ENVIRONMENTALISM
Jonathan Merritt, page 34

The last time you carried your cloth bags into Trader Joe's did you proudly look around in hopes of others noticing your environmental piety? Or are you someone who smirks at "that guy" because you can see through his feeble attempts at cool? In either case is it possible that your foundational reasoning is off base?

Chuck Colson is quoted in the article as saying, "...we are mandated to keep the Garden, to ensure that the beauty and grandeur God has reflected in nature is not despoiled." This quote is a direct reference to the creation mandate given in Genesis 1:28:

God blessed them and said to them, "Be fruitful and increase in number; fill the earth and subdue it. Rule over the fish of the sea and the birds of the air and over every living creature that moves on the ground." (ESV)

Do you agree that this Scripture points to environmentalism being a mandate from God? Defend your answer.

How might your "theology of nature" change by considering environmentalism as a biblical issue?

THAT NASTY MEGAPHONE
Jason Young, page 38

Think about a time in your recent past (or possibly present) when you let pain paralyze you in fear and doubt. Did you play the blame game? How can you re-engage that pain in order to learn or unlearn a valuable life lesson?

What decisions are you currently shying away from because of the pain that you will endure? Which of Jason's five steps do you need to first address in order to enter the pain you have been avoiding?

Do you have a mentor, group, or team with whom you can freely discuss the pain in your life? If not, what are the barriers to discussing your pain? Do you need to ask God to free you from some pride in your life so you can find freedom in authentic relationships?

HIS WILL, NOT YOURS: AN INTERVIEW WITH FRANCIS CHAN
Timothy willard, page 42

Have you ever struggled with God's calling on your life? Knowing God's calling on your life? What do you think about Francis' statement that we should be careful with this sense of calling and focus more on obedience?

Is there a difference between calling and giftedness? Discuss. Have you ever had to lay aside some of your own natural giftedness in order to be all things to all people? (See 1 Corinthians 9:22.)

WHITTLING COMPASSION: HONING A "CONCERN"
Jedd Medefind, page 48

In this article, Jedd talks about the Quaker concept of *concern*, defining it as an invitation to special focus. Has God given you a concern? How can we confirm our sense of calling to engage a concern?

Have you ever been afraid that you have missed God's right path, leaving you in His Plan B or Plan K or even Plan Z for your life? How can we balance the tension between both seeking and waiting for His revealed will?

A FOREVER THRONE
Jonathan Merritt, page 60

What one characteristic would you like to be remembered by in both your life and your ministry? Numbers? Converts? A legacy? What did Billy Graham want to be remembered by?

Can you think of some recent examples where the church has compromised her integrity and given non-Christians fodder for religious skepticism?

FIND ME BIGGER
Jon Adams, page 64

How can we desire God more? How can we learn to make His name great?

Can you connect with Jon's statement that too often his "passion for the Church is connected with the passion for *my own name* to be promoted"? Have you ever found that *your name* is too central in your thinking? What would your ministry look like if your passion for God and making His name great became central in your life?

THE ANTHROPOLOGIST
Timothy Willard, page 68

Are you currently overcome with purposelessness? Or do you feel an urge toward what is beyond the impossible?

Tim says in the article, "We are more than image bearers. We are participants wrapped in holy relationship with God." What is the difference between being an image bearer and a participant in a "holy relationship"? Discuss.

What tension in your life are you currently seeing through the "me lens" instead of the "grace lens"? How might adopting a new lens change how you see your current tensions?

BEYOND RELEVANCE
Gabe Lyons, page 88

What was your initial response when you read the quote from Jon Meacham stating, "While we remain a nation decisively shaped by religious faith our politics and our culture are, in the main, less influenced by movements and arguments of an explicitly Christian character than they were even five years ago." Did you agree with his assessment? Was your initial response that we must fight harder or find another way to influence?

Gabe provides three ways that Christians have historically related to culture–separatism, antagonism, and relevance. Which of these do you most readily identify with? Which do you see as most common in the current evangelical church landscape? Do you agree that there is hopeful change in the landscape? Discuss.

After reading Gabe's definition of "a counterculture for the common good," do you see that existing in your Christian community? Do you naturally lean more toward evangelism or justice? How can you maintain that healthy tension?

The article provides a powerful example of counterculture for the common good through the Season of Service in Portland, Oregon. What similar opportunities may be available in your local context? How might you band together with like-minded leaders to "seek the peace and prosperity" of your city?

FEARLESS:
AN INTERVIEW WITH TAD AGOGLIA
Timothy Willard, page 96

Tad talks about finding your sweet spot and pouring yourself into your dreams. How can we balance the tension between the fear of making those dreams a reality and the desire to make those dreams a reality? Is there an aspect of practicality to go alongside latching onto a dream?

Have you ever had to "consider the cost"? To balance passion and planning?

Do you think that sometimes people understand their unique call to do something, yet they try to build something on passion alone? Planning alone?

SEEK IT LIKE SILVER
John Piper, page 104

Do you struggle with the tension of thinking, feeling, and doing? Which of these are you most naturally bent toward? Which of these should you be doing more of? Do you see them on an even plane in pursuit of Christ or do you see one carrying more weight than the others?

In your church experience is there a history of over-intellectualism or anti-intellectualism? How has that affected the tension between your thinking, feeling, and doing?

Piper uses 1 Cor. 8:1 and John 8:32 to show us that, "Knowing is dangerous. Knowing is liberating. And that is not an isolated paradox." How do these verses show us that knowledge is both dangerous and liberating?

We must live in the tension of "seeking understanding" and "God's giving it." Do you need to seek more? Or do you need to trust more in wisdom from God and not in your own intellectual ability? Discuss.

THAT'S HOT!
Jason Locy & Timothy Willard, page 112

According to Bonhoeffer, how can we seek to be extraordinary in our faith in our culture of self? What does it really mean to be a Christian?

The upside-down culture of the Kingdom teaches us that we shouldn't seek to be known. What should we seek? How can we live "uncommonly"? How can we be extraordinary?

CONTRIBUTORS

JONATHAN ACUFF is the founder of the stuffchris-tianslike.net blog and the author of the book, *Stuff Christians Like*. In the last 12 years he's written brand-ing for clients such as North Point Community Church, The Home Depot, Chick-fil-A, Bose, Staples, and many others. He's a speaker/writer working with the Lampo Group, Dave Ramsey's organization. He lives outside of Nashville with his wife and two daughters.

JON ADAMS grew up in southern California. At five years old, he made a profession of faith that started his journey in Christ. Years later at Wheaton College his perspective on ministry and theology changed dramati-cally. After a brief stint in the public sector Jon felt God calling him to seminary. After two years at Westmin-ster West he went to Chapelgate Presbyterian Church in Ellicott City, Maryland to complete his pastoral in-ternship. There he met and married Liz Anne. Follow-ing his six years serving at Chapelgate, Jon pastored the Perimeter East Church in Atlanta for 10 years. In 2001, God called Jon and his family to plant The Vine Community Church where he currently serves. He and Liz Anne have been married for 25 years and have two lovely daughters, Christy and Melissa.

FRANCIS CHAN was the founder of Cornerstone Church in Simi Valley, where he has been serving for 16 years. Francis and his wife, Lisa, currently feel they are being called to take a step of faith and move to a major city. They will be using the next few months to pray and seek His will as they move from Cornerstone Church.

He is also the Founder of Eternity Bible College and serves on the board of directors for Children's Hunger Fund and World Impact.

Francis does spend time speaking in various places around the world to college-aged adults and pastors and is the au-thor of *Crazy Love* and *Forgotten God*. His commitment is to teach directly from the words of Scripture. It is his passion to see the next generation of American Christians display a much deeper love for Jesus and their neighbors.

MARGARET FEINBERG is a speaker and author of more than a dozen books including the critically ac-claimed *The Organic God* and *The Sacred Echo* and their corresponding six-week Bible studies. Friend her on Facebook or follow her on Twitter @mafeinberg. (www.margaretfeinberg.com)

REGGIE JOINER is the founder and CEO of Orange, a nonprofit organization providing resources and training to help churches maximize their influence on the spiritual growth of the next generation. Orange provides innovative curriculum, resources and training for leaders who work with preschoolers, children, families and students. Reggie is the author of *Think Orange, The Orange Leader Handbook, The Slow Fade,* and *Parenting Beyond Your Capacity.* Reggie and Debbie Joiner live in Cumming, Georgia, and have four grown children: Reggie Paul, Hannah, Sarah, and Rebekah.

TIMOTHY KELLER is the pastor of Redeemer Presbyterian Church in Manhattan, which he started in 1989 with his wife, Kathy, and three young sons. Today, Redeemer has nearly six thousand regular attendees at five services, a host of daughter churches, and is planting churches in large cities throughout the world. He is the *New York Times* bestselling author of *The Reason for God, The Prodigal God,* and *Counterfeit Gods.*

JASON LOCY is the Creative Director of FiveStone, an award winning multi-disciplinary design studio. He lives outside of Atlanta, GA with his wife Heather and three children: Ethan, Christian and Naomi. His first book, *Veneer: Living Deeply in a Surface Society,* is being released through Zondervan/HarperCollins in 2011.

BRAD LOMENICK is Executive Director and key Visionary of Catalyst, a movement of young leaders. Over the last 15 years, he has built a reputation as a key networker and convener of leaders. Prior to running Catalyst, Brad was involved in the growth of the nationally acclaimed *Life@Work* Magazine and did management consulting with Cornerstone Group. More recently he has served in a number of roles for INJOY and now GiANT Impact. For several years after college, he rode horses for a living on a ranch in Colorado, and was even struck by lightning while installing a barbed wire fence, which some believe has given him powers equal to several of the Super Heroes. He hopes maybe someday he can be a professional golfer, or have his own hunting show.

GABE LYONS is the founder of Q and author of *The Next Christians: The Good News About the End of Christian America* (Doubleday, 2010).

BRETT MCCKRACKEN is a Los Angeles-based writer and journalist. A graduate of Wheaton College and UCLA, Brett currently works as managing editor for Biola University's Biola Magazine and is pursuing a Master's in Theology at Talbot School of Theology. He also regularly writes movie reviews and features for Christianity Today, as well as contributing frequently to Relevant magazine. He comments on movies, media, and popular culture issues at his blog, The Search.

JEDD MEDEFIND serves as President of the Christian Alliance for Orphans. The Alliance unites a broad coalition of the nation's leading Christian orphan-serving organizations and a national network of churches committed to caring for orphans. Prior to this role, Jedd served in the White House, leading the Office of Faith-Based and Community Initiatives. In this post, he led reform efforts across government to make the creativity and compassion of local nonprofits central in all Federal efforts to aid the needy, from prisoner reentry to Global AIDS. He has also worked, studied and served in more than thirty countries, with organizations ranging from Price-Waterhouse, Moscow to Christian Life Bangladesh.

JONATHAN MERRITT is a faith and culture writer who has been published in outlets such as *USA Today, Belief-Net,* and *Christianity Today.* He is author of *Green Like God: Unlocking the Divine Plan for Our Planet* (FaithWords, 2010) and teaching pastor at Cross Pointe Church.

BRIAN AND MANDY MILLER lead worship on various occasions for three different churches in Atlanta. Brian serves as the worship pastor at The Vine Community Church, while Mandy sings and leads services at North Point Buckhead, Browns Bridge as well as joining Brian at The Vine. Mandy has also led worship for events like Catalyst and Youth Specialties. The decade before moving to Atlanta, the couple served as worship leaders for several college ministries in Michigan. Their experience with different venues gives them a unique perspective on the heart of worship leading.

MARK A. NOLL (Ph.D., Vanderbilt University) is Francis McAnaney Professor of History at the University of Notre Dame. He is a Fellow of the American Academy of Arts and Sciences. He is advisory editor for Books & Culture and subeditor for the new Religion in Geschichte und Gegenwart. Noll's main academic interests concern the interaction of Christianity and culture in eighteenth- and nineteenth-century Anglo-American societies. He has published articles and reviews on a wide variety of subjects involving Christianity in modern history. Some of his many books include The Civil War as a Theological Crisis, Is the Reformation Over?, The Rise of Evangelicalism: The Age of Edwards, Whitefield and the Wesleys and The Old Religion in a New World.

JOHN ORTBERG is a pastor at Menlo Park Presbyterian Church in Menlo Park, California. He is the bestselling author of When the Game Is Over, It All Goes Back in the Box; The Life You've Always Wanted; and If You Want to Walk on Water, You've Got to Get Out of the Boat. He and his wife Nancy have three children.

JOHN PIPER is the pastor for preaching at Bethlehem Baptist Church in Minneapolis, MN. He grew up in Greenville, SC, and studied at Wheaton College, where he first sensed God's call to enter the ministry. He went on to earn degrees from Fuller Theological Seminary (B.D.) and the University of Munich (D.Theol.). For six years he taught biblical studies at Bethel College in St. Paul, MN, and in 1980 accepted the call to serve as pastor at Bethlehem. John is the author of more than thirty books, and more than twenty-five years of his preaching and teaching is available free at desiringGod.org. John and his wife, Noel, have four sons, one daughter, and an increasing number of grandchildren.

When the band Five Iron Frenzy started a Bible study, little did they know it would morph into a unique church led by pastor **MIKE SARES**. Before he was hoodwinked by the Holy Spirit into working at Scum, Sares served in many roles, including young adult and singles pastor, advertising account executive, salesman, steelworker and high school English teacher. He's been pursuing a M.Div. degree from Denver Seminary for over a decade now. Sares brings his eclectic experience to bear as the senior pastor of an eclectic congregation of artists, punks, skaters, ravers, homeless people and other outcasts at Scum of the Earth Church in Denver, Colorado. To find out more, check out their website at scumoftheearth.net.

ANDY STANLEY is a pastor, communicator, author, and the founder of North Point Ministries (NPM). Since its inception in 1995, North Point Ministries has grown from one campus to three in the Atlanta area and has helped plant over twenty strategic partner churches throughout the United States. Each Sunday, more than twenty thousand adults attend worship services at one of NPM's three campuses: North Point Community Church, Browns Bridge Community Church, and Buckhead Church. Andy's books include the newly released *The Grace of God*, as well as *Communicating for a Change*, *Making Vision Stick*, *Next Generation Leader*, *The Principle of the Path*, and *How Good is Good Enough?* Andy lives in Alpharetta, GA with his wife Sandra and their three children.

In March of 2007 **CARMEN VAUGHT** left her home and work behind to start a journey around the world. Along with a group of students, she traveled to every inhabitable continent over the course of a year, seeking to bring awareness to injustice through photography. Upon their return to the US, they published a book, *Sex & Money: A Global Search for Human Worth*, which shares their photographs and personal encounters with the harsh realities of injustice in our world, specifically highlighting the issue of human trafficking. Carmen is now helping to mobilize others to respond in the fight to end human trafficking.

KAY WARREN is the Founder of the HIV/AIDS initiative at Saddleback Church in Lake Forest, CA. She is an author, international speaker and advocate for orphans and for people infected and affected by HIV and AIDS. Married to Rick Warren, together they founded Saddleback Church in 1980. Kay authored *Dangerous Surrender: What Happens When You Say Yes to God* and co-authored *Foundations*, a systematic theology course used in churches around the world. She has three children and four grandchildren, and lives in Southern California.

CARLOS WHITTAKER is the former service programming director genius for Buckhead Church, a satellite campus of North Point Community Church in Alpharetta, GA. His blog, ragamuffinsoul.com, is (approximately) the most popular blog in the world. And he's recently started the premier creative coaching network.

DALLAS WILLARD is a Southern Baptist minister and author of many theological texts such as *Hearing God, The Spiritual Disciplines,* and *In Search of Guidance*. In 2002, *Renovation of the Heart* was published, receiving *Christianity Today's* 2003 Book Award in the category of Spirituality. *The Divine Conspiracy* was released in 1998 and won *Christianity Today's* "Book of the Year" for 1999. Dallas is widely known as a professor of philosophy at the University of Southern California, where he serves as the Director of the School of Philosophy. He has published many works, most heavily concentrated on extensive translations of Edmund Husserl's early writings.

TIMOTHY WILLARD is an author/writer who has contributed to publications for Catalyst, Chick-fil-A Leadercast, and Q. He is finishing an MA in Christian Thought at Gordon-Conwell Theological Seminary. Timothy is writing his first book *Veneer: Living Deeply In a Surface Society* due out in 2011 with Zondervan/HaperCollins. He lives with his wife Chris and two daughters Lyric and Brielle. He likes his coffee strong and pressed.

JASON YOUNG helps businesses, non-profit organizations, and churches develop people to become influencers. He has multiple degrees and is currently completing his doctoral degree in Leadership Development and Human Behavior with a concentration on those born between 1984-2002. Jason lives in Atlanta, GA with his wife of almost nine years, Stacy. They have a daughter and a son they adopted from South Korea.

NOTES

BOOK EXCERPTS

COMMUNITY FOR THE AGELESS, *page 26*

This article is adapted from *Pure Scum: The Left-Out, the Right-Brained and the Grace of God* by Mike Sares, IVP 2010.

YOU'RE A RACIST, YOU KNOW, *page 28*

Excerpt from *Generous Justice* by Timothy Keller, on sale November 2, 2010 from Dutton. Printed with permission from the publisher.

WHY CHRISTIANS MUST REJECT POP-ENVIRONMENTALISM, *page 34*

Courtesy of FaithWords, a division of Hachette Book Group USA. Used by permission.

WHITTLING COMPASSION, *page 48*

This article originally appeared in *Comment* magazine, the opinion journal of CARDUS: www.cardus.ca/comment

BEYOND RELEVANCE, *page 88*

This article has been adapted from his book, *The Next Christians*, which is on sale now everywhere books are sold. You can connect with Gabe's ongoing work at www.QIdeas.org.

SEEK IT LIKE SILVER, *page 104*

Taken from *Think* by John Piper copyright ©2010. Used by permission of Crossway Books, a publishing ministry of Good News Publishers, Wheaton, Il 60187, www.crossway.org.

THAT'S HOT!, *page 112*

That's Hot is adapted from Tim and Jason's forthcoming book *Veneer: Living Deeply In A Surface Society*, courtesy of Zondervan Publishers. Used by permission.

ENDNOTES

YOU'RE A RACIST, YOU KNOW, *page 28*

[1] See Brian Tierney, *The Idea of Natural Rights: Studies on Natural Rights, Natural Law, and Church Law 1150–1625* (Grand Rapids: Eerdmans, 1997). See chapter 1. See also chapter 2, "A Contest of Narratives," in Nicholas Wolterstorff, *Justice: Rights and Wrongs* (Princeton: Princeton University Press, 2008).

[2] David L. Chappell, *A Stone of Hope: Prophetic Religion and the Death of Jim Crow* (Chapel Hill: University of North Carolina Press, 2004). Also, see Richard W. Willis, *Martin Luther King, Jr., and the Image of God* (New York: Oxford University Press, 2009). This book argues that King and the African-American church drew heavily on the biblical account that all humans are made in "the image of God" and are therefore equal and must be treated with dignity.

[3] Some of the results of this work can be found in the book *Ministries of Mercy: The Call of the Jericho Road* (Grand Rapids: Zondervan, 1986).

[4] Harvie M. Conn, *Evangelism: Doing Justice and Preaching Grace* (Grand Rapids: Zondervan, 1982).

[5] Elaine Scarry, *On Beauty and Being Just* (Princeton: Princeton University Press, 1999).

WHY CHRISTIANS MUST REJECT POP-ENVIRONMENTALISM, *page 34*

1 Mimi Spencer, "Is Green the New Black?" Observer, April 15, 2007, www.guardian.co.uk/lifeandstyle/2007/apr/15/fashion.features1/print.

2 Marcelle Hopkins, "Green Is the New Black: Eco-Fashion Goes Mainstream," November 28, 2006, http://jscms.jrn.columbia.edu/cns/2006-11-28/hopkins-ecofashion. (Also see http://www.azcentral.com/ent/pop/articles/1129ecofashion1129.html)

3 Adam Lashinsky, "Be Green—Everybody's Doing It," CNN Money.com, July 12, 2006, http://money.cnn.com/2006/07/12/news/economy/pluggedin_lashinsky.fortune/ index.htm?section=money_topstories

4 Charles Colson and Ellen Santilli Vaughn, *The Body*, W Publishing Group, 1996, p. 197.

A FOREVER THRONE, *page 60*

1 William C. Martin, *A Prophet With Honor: The Billy Graham Story* (Harper Perennial, 1992), p. 603.

FIND ME BIGGER, *page 64*

1 C.S. Lewis, *Prince Caspian* (San Francisco: HarperCollinsPublishers, 2008), 141.

REARTICULATING THE DIVINE, *page 80*

1 Dick Staub, *The Culturally Savvy Christian: A Manifesto for Deepening Faith and Enriching Popular Culture in an Age of Christianity-Lite* (San Francisco: Jossey-Bass, 2007), 72.

SEEK IT LIKE SILVER, *page 104*

1 John Dillenberger, ed. *Martin Luther: Selections from His Writings* (Garden City, NY: Doubleday, 1961), 12.

2 John Piper, *The Justification of God: A Theologicanl and Exegetical and Theological Study of Romans 9:1-23* (1983; repr. Grand Rapids: Baker, 1993).

3 Mark Noll, *The Scandal of the Evangelical Mind* (Grand Rapids: Eerdmans, 1994), 3.

4 Harry Blamires, *The Christian Mind: How Should a Christian Think?* (London: SPCK, 1963), 6.

5 J. P. Moreland, *Love God with All Your Mind: The Role of Reason in the Life of the Soul* (Colorado Springs: NavPress, 1997), 19–40.

6 Os Guinness, *Fit Bodies Fat Minds: Why Evangelicals Don't Think and What to Do About It* (Grand Rapids: Baker, 1994). "At root, evangelical anti-intellectualism is both a scandal and a sin. It is a scandal in the sense of being an offense and a stumbling block that needlessly hinders serious people from considering the Christian faith and coming to Christ. It is a sin because it is a refusal, contrary to the first of Jesus' two great commandments, to love the Lord our God with our minds" (pp. 10–11).

7 R. C. Sproul, "Burning Hearts Are Not Nourished by Empty Heads," Christianity Today (September 3, 1982), 100.

8 Noll, 132.

9 Ibid., 3. "An extraordinary range of virtues is found among the sprawling throngs of evangelical Protestants in North America, including great sacrifice in spreading the message of salvation in Jesus Christ, open-hearted generosity to the needy, heroic personal exertion on behalf of troubled individuals, and the unheralded sustenance of countless church and parachurch communities."

10 Benjamin Warfield, "The Religious Life of Theological Students," in The Princeton Theology, ed. Mark Noll (Grand Rapids: Baker, 1983), 263.

THAT'S HOT, *page 112*

1 Daniel Boorstin, *The Image: A Guide to Pseudo-Events in America* (New York: Vintage Books, 1961), 57.

2 Neal Gabler, *Life, The Movie: How Entertainment Conquered Reality* (New York: Vintage Books, 1998), 146.

3 http://www.tampabay.com/features/media/article1016296.ece

4 Bonnie "Prince" Billy, Love Comes to Me.

5 Klauss Bochmeuhl, *The Christian way of Living* (Vancouver: Regent College Publishing, 1997), 57.

6 Chris Hedges, *Empire of Illusion* (New York: Nations Books, 2009),16.

7 http://www.wired.com/culture/lifestyle/magazine/16-08/howto_allison

8 http://www.wired.com/culture/lifestyle/magazine/16-08/howto_allison?currentPage=3

9 Craig M. Gay, *The Way of the Modern World: Or Why It's Tempting to Live as if God Doesn't Exist* (Grand Rapids: Wm. B. Eerdmans Publishing Company, 1998), 196. Gray quotes Martin Buber from Thomas F. Torrance's *God and Rationality* (Oxford: Oxford Press, 1971), 29.

10 Fyodor Dostoyevsky, *The Grand Inquisitor* (Indianapolis: Hackett Publishing Co., 1993), 28.

11 The words of Jesus were paraphrased in this section by the authors. They originate in Matthew 4:1-11 (NIV).

12 Dietrich Bonhoeffer, *The Cost of Discipleship* (Macmillan Publishing Company, 1963), 69.

13 Ibid., 175.

14 Ibid.

CATALYST® WEST CATALYSTWESTCOAST.COM
888.334.6569

A convergence of next generation leaders

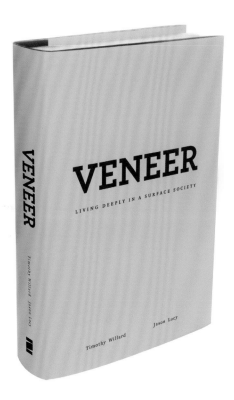